TIM JARVIS
MAWSON
LIFE AND DEATH IN ANTARCTICA

THE MIEGUNYAH PRESS

The Miegunyah Press

This is number one hundred in the
second numbered series of the
Miegunyah Volumes
made possible by the
Miegunyah Fund
established by bequests
under the wills of
Sir Russell and Lady Grimwade.

'Miegunyah' was the home of
Mab and Russell Grimwade
from 1911 to 1955.

THE MIEGUNYAH PRESS
An imprint of Melbourne University Publishing Limited
187 Grattan Street, Carlton, Victoria 3053, Australia
mup-info@unimelb.edu.au
www.mup.com.au

First published 2008
Text © Tim Jarvis and Film Australia 2008
Design and typography © Melbourne University Publishing Ltd 2008

This book is copyright. Apart from any use permitted under the *Copyright Act 1968* and subsequent amendments, no part may be reproduced, stored in a retrieval system or transmitted by any means or process whatsoever without the prior written permission of the publisher.

Every attempt has been made to locate the copyright holders for material quoted in this book. Any person or organisation that may have been overlooked or misattributed may contact the publisher.

Designed and typeset by Nada Backovic
Printed in Australia by Impact Printing

National Library of Australia Cataloguing-in-Publication entry

    Jarvis, Tim.

    Mawson : life and death in Antarctica / author, Tim Jarvis.

    9780522854862 (pbk.)

    Mawson, Douglas, Sir, 1882–1958.
    Jarvis, Tim—Travel—Antarctica.
    Australasian Antarctic Expedition (1911–1914).
    Australians—Antarctica.
    Historical reenactments.
    Antarctica—Description and travel.
    Antarctica—Discovery and exploration—Australian.

919.8904092

Foreword

I grew up in the UK, where the term 'polar hero' was usually reserved for Captain Robert Falcon Scott. I had known about his exploits since childhood. The pathos of his death, and even more so those of his team, touched me, as it did thousands.

It wasn't until I was preparing to migrate to Australia myself that a friend told me of Douglas Mawson's extraordinary story. Perhaps blinded by Scott's celebrity, Mawson's exploits had been largely forgotten in the UK, despite the fact that Mawson had been born in Britain.

This only whetted my appetite to tell the story—somehow.

Amazingly, the question of how to tell the story was solved soon after my arrival in Australia. I was given a pile of proposals to review while working in development at the ABC. As I went through them, I picked up one that had on the cover the familiar picture of a craggy-faced Mawson in his woollen balaclava.

I held in my hands a proposal for a film that not only told the Mawson story, but did so in a way I instantly saw could be more powerful and visceral than a mere description of events. In the hyper-competitive world of modern television, something special was needed to tell the story—and here it was.

Producer Richard Dennison, a veteran of the adventure film genre, had come up with the key in the lock. That key was Tim Jarvis and his bold plan to retrace Mawson's footsteps, in order to really experience what the Far Eastern Sledging Party expedition of 1912–13 had been like. I was then fortunate enough to join Film Australia, with a brief to produce high quality films on Australian history. From the start of my new role, we began to work on the enormous logistical and safety challenges that a trip to the frozen continent would bring.

Alongside Richard Dennison, we needed a first-rate production team, and found exactly that in director Malcolm McDonald, line producer Perry Stapleton and cinematographer Wade Fairley. We also teamed up with the Australian Antarctic Division, without which nothing would have been possible.

Finally, there was Mawson's contemporary 'co-star' in the drama: the man who was actually going to make the trek.

Tim Jarvis is a remarkable person; a true renaissance man whose interest in the world and its environment is combined with a powerful inner need to discover his personal limits. He has walked solo to the South Pole, and did it more quickly than any man in history. Equally, he can be found trekking in steaming jungles, on mountain ascents and working on development projects in remote areas. He is an expert on Australia's current drought. Tim now increasingly is confronting what I think is an even more challenging frontier: the boardrooms of big business, where he educates influential leaders about climate change.

When I met Tim, I could see his personal charisma and integrity would make for a wonderful film.

But *Mawson: Life and Death in Antarctica* is about more than Tim and his colleague John Stoukalo's polar adventure. As Executive Producer of Film Australia's 'Making History' initiative, I was determined that the film would also provide an insight into Australian history at a critical time in this country's development.

Just a decade after Federation, Australia was a confident, independently minded young nation. We wanted to be something in the world, and Mawson's expedition, as a purely Australian endeavour, came to symbolise that. Mawson, who turned down a job on Scott's ill-fated race to the South Pole, was an able politician who exploited Australia's new nationalism in his efforts to raise funds from the social elite of the day for his own expedition.

Having raised those funds, Mawson bought the *Aurora*, in which he would make the voyage south. What happened next is the subject of the television documentary *Mawson: Life and Death in Antarctica*, the subject of this book and the story of Tim's extraordinary journey into the ice.

You'll have to read on to discover how things turned out, but there is one result I can give away. When shown on UK television, the documentary was watched by around a million viewers and did much to re-awaken long overdue British recognition of Douglas Mawson as a hero of polar exploration.

In Australia, we are generally more familiar with Douglas Mawson's achievements. Now you can also experience what Tim Jarvis and his team achieved by retracing Mawson's amazing journey.

Alex West
Executive Producer, *Mawson: Life and Death in Antarctica*

Contents

Introduction		1
1	Arrival	19
2	The Plateau	41
3	Stopka	65
4	Wind Power	83
5	Losing a Friend	103
6	Alone on the Shores of the World	125
7	False Start	149
8	Climbing	161
9	Iceberg Alley	185
10	'Just Have One More Try—It's Dead Easy to Die'	199
Epilogue: So This is the End		215
Appendix: Antarctica under Threat		228
Picture Credits		236
Acknowledgements		238

Introduction

In 1912 Douglas Mawson and two colleagues—Belgrave Ninnis, a British army officer, and Xavier Mertz, a Swiss doctor—set off on the Far Eastern Sledging Party, a journey into previously uncharted territory to fill in a missing piece of the Antarctic jigsaw, a literal blank on the map. It was a journey that Mawson suspected would be dangerous, given the nature of the heavily crevassed terrain he anticipated encountering. It was for this reason that he chose to lead the expedition himself rather than assign the task to one of his men.

It became one of the greatest journeys of polar survival: terrible circumstances befell Mawson. The death of both of his colleagues—Ninnis a victim of a crevasse fall and Mertz dying of unknown causes—left Mawson alone and facing death up on the icy vastness of the Antarctic plateau. To save himself, he battled ferocious winds, subzero temperatures, unfathomable crevasses and horrific injury, and finally stumbled into camp against the longest possible odds. Such was his physical state on arrival that he was greeted by the words 'Which one are you?': the malnourished, frostbitten shell of a man was unrecognisable as Mawson.

Previous page: *A wall of blue: an old iceberg gradually crumbling into the sea;*
opposite: *The face tells the story: Mawson in a typical pose.*

For many people today, the Mawson story is often more a collection of images: men lost in blinding blizzards, dogs being eaten, a heroic battle against terrible cold and loneliness, and human sacrifice, with an undercurrent of controversy brought about by talk of cannibalism. For those who are more familiar with the story of Mawson's lone survival, it is one that inspires: a journey of survival against all the odds and a defining moment in an already full and varied life. Mawson's is perhaps one of the least recognised but most remarkable stories of human endeavour and polar survival.

Mawson was a contemporary of Robert Falcon Scott, Ernest Shackleton and Roald Amundsen back in the heroic era of polar exploration, in the early years of the twentieth century. It is perhaps because of the events unfolding around him at the time that his incredible journey in 1913 is not afforded the recognition that it deserves. The year of 1909 had been an amazing one for polar exploration: Robert Peary reached the North Pole and Shackleton the furthest south towards the South Pole, the latter forced to turn around just 156 kilometres short of his goal. The Norwegian Amundsen had the unconquered South Pole in his sights and eventually reached it in late 1911. His stunning achievement was overshadowed by the death of Scott and all of his men in early 1912 on their return journey, after being beaten by Amundsen to their goal. Perhaps the final act in the heroic era was Shackleton's, saving all of his men from certain death by undertaking a truly incredible journey of 1300 kilometres in a small rowing boat to reach a remote whaling station on South Georgia and raise the alarm. The outbreak of World War I, which destroyed the innocence and idealism of a generation, marked the end of this heroic era.

Mawson was an integral part of this polar tapestry. He had been a member of Shackleton's Nimrod expedition of 1907–09 and was in the first party to scale the Antarctic volcano Erebus in 1908. As Shackleton attempted to become the first person to reach the South Geographic Pole, Mawson reached the South Magnetic Pole along with Edgeworth David, an Australian, and Alistair Mackay, a Scot, undertaking the longest ever sledge journey in the process. Declining an offer to be a member of Scott's Discovery Expedition of 1911, Mawson pulled together his own expedition (the Australasian Antarctic Expedition, or AAE) with ambitious exploration and scientific goals, setting off in early December 1911 from Hobart. As Mawson was setting up his base at the place he named Commonwealth Bay in March 1912, Scott and the last two of his men, Henry 'Birdie' Bowers and Dr Edward Wilson, were dying only a

few kilometres short of their final food depot, cold and alone somewhere out on the Ross Ice Shelf. Mawson went on to undertake a huge program of scientific and geographical discovery in the two years of the AAE—an achievement in itself—but it was as sole survivor of the Far Eastern Sledging Party journey, which claimed the lives of both of his colleagues, that his place in the polar annals was secured.

How do I describe my reasons for wanting to re-enact this treacherous polar journey, to put myself through a similar ordeal? They are not straightforward. I did not begin with a blinding flash of inspiration or some feeling of predetermination to attempt that which Mawson had done. Rather, it was a slow-burn realisation that began when I first arrived in Adelaide in 1997.

Above left: *Belgrave Ninnis, the young British Army officer, in full military dress;*
above right: *Dr Xavier Mertz, Swiss ski champion.*

Mawson and the Australasian Antarctic Expedition

Mawson was born in 1882 in Yorkshire, England. In 1884 his family moved to Sydney, where he studied mining engineering, graduating in 1902.

In 1905 Mawson was appointed lecturer in mineralogy and petrology at the University of Adelaide where he became interested in the glacial geology of South Australia. This in turn led to his interest in Antarctica where such glacial processes were still at work. In November 1907, Mawson asked Sir Ernest Shackleton, who was visiting Adelaide on his way to Antarctica, if he might join him and he was duly appointed, serving as physicist of the expedition.

In March 1908, together with his mentor Professor Edgeworth David from Sydney University, Mawson was a member of the first team to climb Mount Erebus, and the following summer, together with David and Mackay, he became the first to reach the South Magnetic Pole—a man-haul of more than 2000 kilometres. David said of Mawson, 'We really have in him an Australian Nansen [famed Norwegian explorer], of infinite resource, splendid physique, astonishing indifference to frost'.

In 1909 Scott was planning his Terra Nova expedition and invited Mawson to join his South Pole sledging party. This did not interest Mawson, who was a scientist first and an explorer second. Mawson began the process of instead planning his own bid to launch what was to become the Australasian Antarctic Expedition.

After massive effort, the expedition was finally organised and sailed on the *Aurora* for Antarctica in December 1911. The goal of the AAE was to 'investigate as far as possible, the stretch of prospective but practically unknown Antarctic coast extending almost 2000 miles [3200 km] in an east and west direction between the farthest west of the Terra Nova [Scott's British Expedition of 1910] and the farthest east of the Gauss [German Antarctic Expedition of 1902]'. The program

George V Land — Far Eastern Sledging Party journey of 1912–13

1:350,000
polar stereographic projection

easternmost point of expedition

Ninnis Glacier

glacier extents, 1913

Mertz Glacier

Cape Denison

Cook Ice Shelf

Cape Hudson

150°E 67°S 145°E 66°S 68°S

of work included the scientific examination of Macquarie Island, a study of the ocean floor en route between Australia and Antarctica and detailed observations in magnetism, geology, biology and meteorology in Antarctica.

Three bases were established: one at the subantarctic Macquarie Island, which, apart from its scientific work, served as a radio relay station; Main Base under Mawson at a place christened Commonwealth Bay; and Western Base on the Shackleton Ice Shelf under Frank Wild. Major scientific work was pursued in a range of areas from the bases.

Eighteen men spent the winter of 1912 at Main Base, the winter quarters, at Cape Denison in Commonwealth Bay. The next summer, five exploratory sledging journeys were undertaken from here, with the Far Eastern Sledging Party journey being the most dangerous, given the nature of the crevassed terrain it would likely cross.

As leader of the expedition, Mawson took charge of this journey, not out of a desire for a challenge but because he felt it was his duty.

It is this journey that I and John Stoukalo sought to re-create and about which this book is written. It was one that saw Mawson arrive back at the Main Base alone and terribly malnourished on 8 February 1913, just hours after the *Aurora* left for home with most of the men. He was nursed back to health while staying on with six volunteers for an unplanned second year at Main Base. Mawson documented the journey in his book, *The Home of the Blizzard*. He was subsequently knighted for his achievements in leading the Australian Antarctic Expedition—an expedition that succeeded in establishing Australia's territorial claim over 40 per cent of Antarctica.

Above: *The route of the Far Eastern Sledging Party.*

At that time I had no more than a passing notion of Mawson. Interestingly, on closer examination we had some characteristics in common. We were both born in England—Mawson in Yorkshire and I just across the Pennines in Manchester—and we were also born within two calendar days of one another (although 84 years apart), Mawson on 5 May and I on 7 May, making us both stubborn Taureans. Mawson moved as a young boy to Sydney with his parents and then to Adelaide to work as a lecturer in geology at the University of Adelaide, and I too went to Adelaide to work in the field of earth sciences 90 years later, as an environmental scientist. We were even similar in height, at 1.93 and 1.96 metres.

Above left: *An iceberg mirrored in the ocean;*
above right: *Pack ice stretches to the horizon, the flat expanse broken only by the occasional iceberg.*

But a decade ago these similarities would not have meant much to me. With one Arctic trip under my belt, I was enjoying the warmer climes of Adelaide, having decided to focus on environmental work for a while. But Adelaide was steeped in the legacy of Mawson and, through a process of osmosis, I found myself considering another polar journey, this time south, although the precise goal was not initially clear.

Before long, however, I started wondering about the possibility of an attempt to retrace Mawson's survival journey, partly as an ambitious goal to aim for, and partly to see how I measured up. The more I discovered about Mawson, the more I liked the idea, but the sales pitch wasn't an easy one. If I was to be true to his original journey, I needed to have

two people to accompany me and have them both die agonising deaths, surprisingly not a popular proposition with potential candidates. Ultimately, I instead planned to attempt to cross Antarctica, and I somehow felt he would have approved of my breaking new ground for the reasons of real discovery rather than for the purpose of retracing his footsteps.

What followed was a two-year effort to be the first to cross the Antarctic continent unsupported, pulling all the provisions needed for the journey behind me in a sled with a crippling 220-kilogram load. It was a journey of self-discovery during which I pushed myself harder than I had ever thought possible and one from which I returned a changed person in early 2000, four months after setting off. Reaching the Pole in a record time meant that even someone as privately self-critical as I could see that I had achieved something noteworthy. I was eager to find out more about the powerful alter ego that had emerged in me in response to the challenges posed by my journey.

I had toiled to the South Pole in forty-seven days, two days faster than any unsupported team had ever managed before. My achievements begged comparison with the journeys of my childhood heroes, but my achievement sat uncomfortably with me—I wondered whether it was really comparable with the journeys of old, where the boats were wooden but the men who travelled in them were iron through and through. I took comfort in the notion that the bastion of 'doing things the old way' still existed, even as I made plans to break down this bastion. And so the notion of undertaking a journey not as a modern explorer with breathable synthetics, Kevlar and dehydrated meals but as an explorer of old with heavy wooden sled, animal pelts and heroic-era stoicism hooked me. If it could be achieved, then truly there would be no more to do. Perhaps then I could stand up and be counted.

As I had walked the final steps into the Pole in late 1999, I realised I had taken an almost identical time to that of Mawson on his journey from the moment when Ninnis died until he reached a food cache, alone and starving, back in 1913. On my South Pole journey I had eaten some 29 400 kilojoules a day and experienced a weight loss of more than 17 kilograms. For Mawson, it had been far, far worse.

Previous page: *Mertz, Ninnis and HD Murphy en route with stores to Aladdin's Cave;*
opposite: *Mertz with the dog team, fan-hitched to the sled, sledging up the ice slopes.*

When I arrived back in Adelaide in early 2000, I also realised that for the past few years I had been on two journeys. The first was a literal one down in the snow and ice while the second was one of self-discovery inextricably linked with Mawson and the inspiration that his journey of survival provided. Suddenly it felt to me that my coming to Adelaide may not have been entirely coincidental and that attempting the Far Eastern Sledging Party expedition was a logical conclusion for my bigger journey. It would be the ultimate challenge, to travel with a companion the equivalent distance—from where Ninnis died to where Mawson found food left for him by an advance rescue party—a journey of almost 500 kilometres across some of the most inhospitable terrain in the world using the same clothes, technology, equipment and starvation rations as Mawson and Mertz had available to them after Ninnis' death. My companion in his role as Mertz would 'die' and be extracted at the same point as Mertz died—after we had covered 320 kilometres or twenty-five days had elapsed, whichever came first. It would be a journey requiring massive mental and physical effort to realise, and the coming together of a unique set of players.

Finding someone who was prepared to accompany me on such a challenging undertaking, and 'die' halfway through, was not easy. My companion needed a unique set of skills: resourcefulness, stoicism, good climbing ability in the event of a crevasse fall, cold tolerance, good mechanical skills and preferably prior Antarctic experience. After a year of looking, my business partner, Dick Dennison, introduced me to a Russian friend of his who now lived in Sydney: Evgeny 'John' Stoukalo. I knew we had our man. Formerly of Vladivostok, John was ex–Russian military, an excellent climber, had grown up in Siberia, was a competitive cross-country ski racer and worked as an aeronautical engineer. Within days he had been recruited onto the team. We toasted his inclusion in the Russian way: 'to the success of our terrible deal', the Russian equivalent of 'break a leg'.

To make the project viable, it had to be filmed, and we needed a high-calibre film team. Malcolm McDonald was put in charge of filming. He had a wealth of experience in documentary and drama genres, including being second unit director on *Master and Commander*, which starred Russell Crowe. He was a great choice. Supporting him was Wade Fairley as cameraman, with his broad polar experience: he was responsible for bringing us spectacular images of emperor penguins as part of the BBC's *Planet Earth* series. His partner, Frederique, was responsible for sound, and Dr David Tingay, an experienced Himalayan climber, was the expedition doctor.

While the expedition that John and I undertook was as similar as we could possibly make it to Mawson's, there were major differences. Mawson and Mertz embarked, as we did, on a journey of survival, but, in their case, failure meant death. Ultimately we knew that with a film crew and doctor travelling parallel to us, seldom more than a day's motorised travel away, our chances of dying were greatly reduced. For Mawson, particularly when he was on his own, stopping and giving up meant death; for us, stopping would have been relatively easy, knowing that we had support on the plateau. Mawson and Mertz couldn't stop; we, assuming the weather was good, could have been reunited with the crew inside a day—a fact I suspected would make it harder, in many respects, to keep going. It gave us something of a false sense of security too, as, in the event of our tent failing in a blizzard, in the zero visibility the film crew may not have been able to get to us in time.

Our route was different from that of Mawson and Mertz, as the logistics of travelling over the same ground proved impossible to arrange, given King George V Land's distance from the nearest point to where an Australian Antarctic Division ship could drop us off. I had no issue with this, as the ground over which Mawson travelled in 1912 and 1913 was long gone anyway; the ice moves seawards from Antarctica's interior at a rate of several hundred metres a year. It would have been impossible for us to walk over the same literal ground and cross the same crevasses as he did.

I viewed our expedition a bit like a control experiment, much as a scientist eliminates variables to help isolate the real causes of the subject under investigation. We kept as much as we could the same as it had been for Mawson, and if, by not eating dog livers, we did not end up in the same awful physical state as Mawson, it would speak volumes about the relevance of the vitaminosis theory (whether or not Mawson and Mertz poisoned themselves by consuming the livers of some of the sled dogs). Whatever happened, I would not give myself credit for having done what Mawson did, but would come as close as was possible in the modern era.

This book recounts what happened on that journey: a journey on which, while trying to get closer to knowing Mawson and what happened to him and Mertz almost a century ago down on the lonely Antarctic ice cap, I also came to learn so much more about myself.

Opposite: *Talking about what we are going to do is easy—doing it is another matter.*

Antarctic Science

Antarctica is the fifth largest continent and, with an area of more than 14 million square kilometres, is almost twice the size of Australia. About 98 per cent of Antarctica is covered by the Antarctic ice cap, which contains approximately 75 to 80 per cent of the world's fresh water. The ice has an average thickness of approximately 2 kilometres with the thickest ice being some 4700 metres thick. The total volume of ice in the cap is so massive—at 28 million cubic kilometres—that, if the weight of the ice were removed, scientists estimate that the underlying rock would rise on average by a kilometre. In winter, the sea ice around Antarctica grows at the rate of 100 000 square kilometres a day, doubling the size of the continent.

The weight of the ice at the top of the high ground or 'dome' near Antarctica's centre is so great that gravity makes the underlying ice deform and spread downhill. The rate of movement varies from less than a metre a year at the South Pole to several hundred metres per year near the edges. Eventually, the ice forms floating 'ice shelves' or valley glaciers, from which icebergs calve off into the ocean. The largest of these broke off in the 1950s and measured 360 kilometres long by 120 kilometres wide—about the size of Belgium!

The world's largest ice shelves are the Ross and Ronne ice shelves in Antarctica. They range in thickness from 100 to 1000 metres, with only about 10 per cent of their visible ice being above the surface as they float in the ocean. Scott called the Ross Ice Shelf the great ice barrier, because it appeared to him to be a continuous impenetrable ice cliff hundreds of kilometres long. Its ocean cliff-face is in fact some 600 kilometres long.

Antarctica is the only continent never to have had an indigenous population of humans because it is so extreme. It is the coldest, windiest and highest continent. It is also the driest continent, with the driest parts having had no precipitation for 250 000 years. Antarctica's average height is 2300 metres

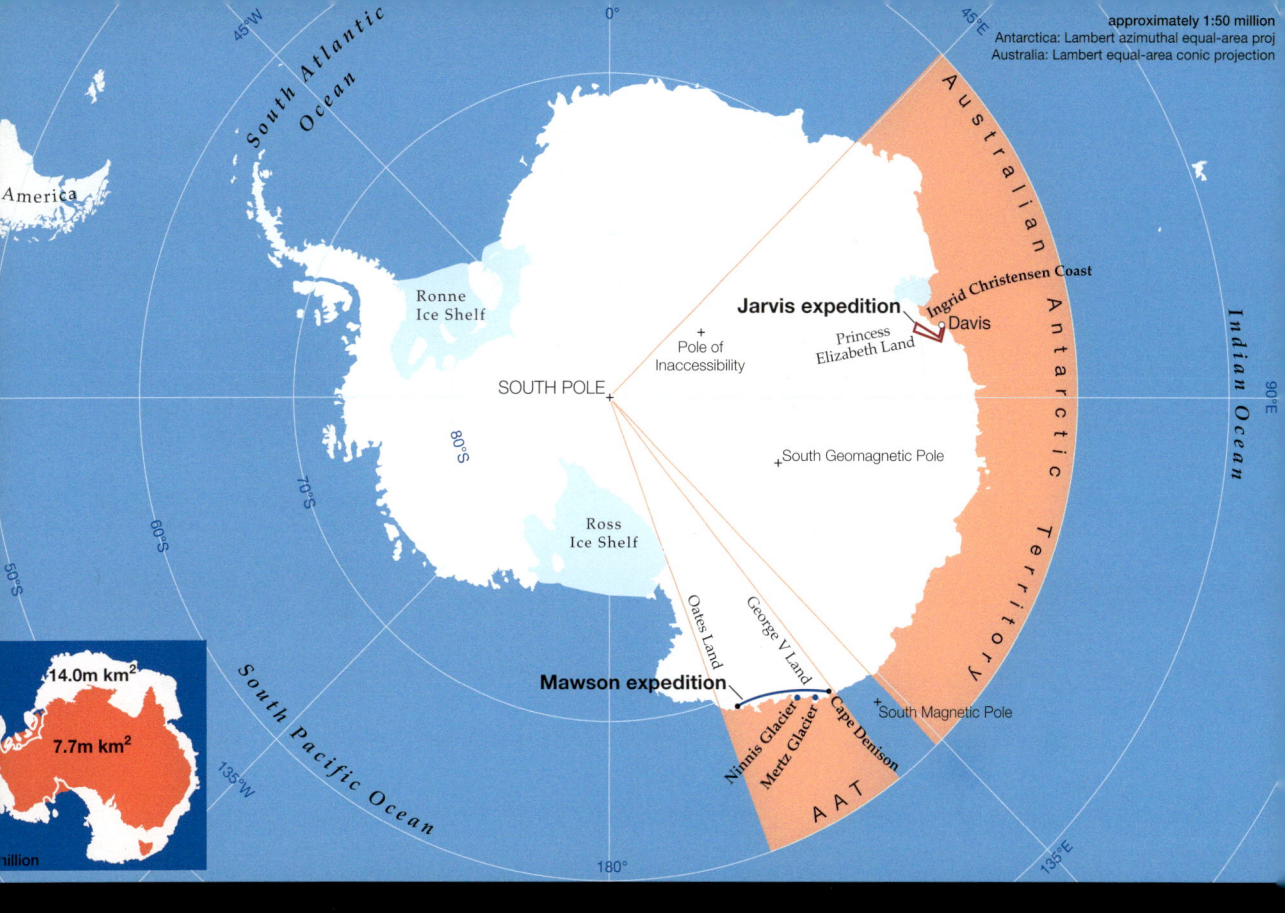

above sea level; the coldest temperature recorded is –89.4°C; and the strongest winds—the katabatic winds around the edges of the continent—can blow at up to 300 kilometres an hour. These are the winds that caused Mawson to name Commonwealth Bay 'The Home of the Blizzard'.

Antarctica has four Poles: the Geomagnetic and Magnetic Poles, the Geographic South Pole and the Pole of Inaccessibility. The Pole of Inaccessibility is the point on average farthest from any coast, whereas the Geographic South Pole is the true South Pole and, with the North Pole, is one of the two points on the surface of Earth through which the Earth's axis of rotation passes. The South Pole today sits at an altitude of 2835 metres above sea level, although the ice here accounts for more than 95 per cent of the height—the underlying 'land' surface is actually near sea level. The Amundsen–Scott Base is located at the South Pole. I achieved the fastest time for an unsupported journey to the Pole when I walked to this base in 1999.

Above: *My route, compared with that of Mawson's journey*

1 Arrival

An invisible baton had been passed to the birds of the Antarctic by their northern cousins, who had turned back, their job of accompanying us as far south as the Antarctic convergence done. For more than a week, ice floes had been speckled with Adelie penguins, while now, instead of the birds that we had seen since leaving Tasmania, wandering albatross and terns wheeled overhead.

The increasingly loud throb of both engines told me that the pack ice had been thickening for some time and that Antarctica must lurk just below the horizon. Its first appearance was still awe inspiring: massive white ice cliffs 100 metres high rising vertically from the dark ocean, and a steep slope of ice leading inland towards the pole thousands of metres higher and 2500 kilometres further south. The ship's mate reckoned we could see 100 kilometres inland from our vantage point off the coast, due to the unique combination of the gradual increase in height from the tops of the cliffs south towards the Pole that offset the curve of the Earth and the crystal-clear, unpolluted air.

Previous page: *Skuas: Antarctica's number one feathered predator.*

Life on ship had been a succession of delicious meals served at rigorously observed mealtimes, training in the ship's gym and the weekly survival drills. The drills exposed us to the icy wind up on deck, rudely reminding us of how, below deck, it was all too easy to forget where we were: deep in the remote Southern Ocean. The safety drills seemed particularly incongruous given what we were about to undertake: deliberately and counter-intuitively depriving ourselves of sufficient food and shelter up on the cold polar plateau and seeing what happened.

The scale of the terrain we passed just off the Antarctic coast defied superlatives. Icebergs kilometres wide, with white and turquoise pack ice metres thick, forced the engines to consume 1000 litres of diesel per hour to push their way through. The temperature had become a lot colder too, the decks now coated in a surreal wind-blown crust of icicles—the result of frozen spray from our rough ocean passage. John and I stood on deck marvelling at the beauty of the scene. I felt inspired. John did too; it reminded him of life back home in the Siberian winter. Specifically, he recalled his method for making moonshine where an alcoholic substance could be 'distilled' by turning the bottle containing it upside down and allowing it to drip slowly. In subzero conditions any water in the solution quickly formed an icicle, leaving pure alcohol as the remaining liquid still dripping from the bottle. That was John all round: ingenuity with

Previous page: *Studying an iceberg: on some days the ocean was as calm as a millpond amongst the pack ice;* below: *On board ship, with the Ingrid Christensen Coast in the background;*
opposite top: *The* Aurora Australis: *capable of pushing through pack ice 3 metres thick;*
opposite bottom: *Next stop Antarctica.*

a classic Russian sense of humour based on deadpan understatement. Just the man for this expedition, where lateral thought, problem-solving ability and stoicism were going to be high on the agenda.

The ship had been moving slowly for a while and it wasn't long before we finally came to a halt in the bay opposite Davis Base, named after John King Davis, skipper to both Mawson's and Shackleton's expeditions. The captain killed the engines and with that our momentum stopped instantly. We had arrived.

We had mixed emotions on arriving, our mood veering crazily from excitement and a broader sense of purpose to concern and a quiet fear about the immensity of what we were planning to subject ourselves to. Often John and I would feel insular, retreating into our shells, trying to put any thought of what lay ahead out of our minds; at other times, the thought of it excited us and we felt ready for the challenge. Overall, I was elated to arrive at Davis, as arrival symbolised the success of having pulled the expedition together. I also welcomed the purity of Antarctica with its ability to strip back life to the bare essentials: survival in a place where

Above left: *Our trail through thickening pack ice, with icebergs in the background;*
above right: *Recently broken, metre-thick pack ice. The* Aurora Australis *used both engines when travelling through thicker ice such as this;*
opposite: *Everywhere is north from here: John in Cossack pose.*

nature presents itself in all its austere beauty and on a massive scale. More than anything, I relished the opportunity to experience that more resourceful side of my personality that such conditions brought out in me. At times though I wasn't sure precisely what I felt. I had well and truly had enough of ship life and its sedentary living, plentiful food and bureaucratic processes, but the prospect of being starving, cold and alone up on the plateau still felt too alien to comprehend.

The 2-kilometre journey from the ship to the base must rank as one of the shortest chopper journeys in history: we landed at the Davis helipad seemingly seconds after taking off. Davis was a strange place, a crossroads at the bottom of the world with everything in a state of flux, people buzzing around with a sense of anticipation, loading and unloading kitbags and scientific equipment, embracing, laughing, chatting noisily and going through the handover ritual that had repeatedly taken place since 1957 when Davis Base first opened for business. Dishevelled 'winterers'—the small number of men and women who had stayed at Davis for fifteen months, four of which had been in complete darkness—were going through the bittersweet experience of having their isolation come to an abrupt end, with the newcomers arriving with the latest news and mail from the outside world and to take over their jobs.

John and I sat in the mess hall, quietly anonymous amidst the hustle and bustle, eating what was likely to be our last decent meal before our starvation diet of kangaroo jerky, lard and sledging biscuits. The weather was looking good for us to fly immediately up to the Skiway, a remote supply building 30 kilometres from the base, on the fringes of the plateau where our man-haul journey would begin.

John and I looked at one another with an impending sense of what was coming and made small talk. It was a disorienting time and hard to keep feelings of doubt far from the mind. Suddenly, after years of planning and weeks aboard ship with its frustratingly slow pace of life, I felt I was being rushed, that I was mentally and psychologically ill prepared, and I was concerned that some critical piece of the jigsaw had been forgotten. Frank, the head of the three-man chopper team at Davis, leaned over us, interrupting our meal and informing us it was time to go.

Opposite: *Adelie penguins on their slowly melting home.*

We walked through the buildings of Davis, a multicoloured selection of workshops and laboratories, in the direction of the helicopter pads. The choppers were warming up. Our larger items of gear had been slung underneath. All that remained now was for us to join them.

As we lifted off, the vastness of the plateau immediately revealed itself beyond the Vestfold Hills to the south, a small, snowless chain of low mountains that had emerged from beneath the ice with the recent retreat of the plateau. From our vantage point, they looked like a dyke holding back the immensity of the plateau's ice, which sat omnipotent behind them, far thicker than the Vestfolds' highest peak.

The peaks and ribbon lakes of the Vestfolds were behind us within ten minutes of flying, as we reached the 600-metre-thick steep slope of ice that marked the fringe of the plateau. A massive uprush of wind kicked the chopper violently sideways, producing a classically understated reaction from Frank. 'Interesting thermal activity—watch out', he warned the pilot of the chopper behind us. I thought it would be a shame to die in a helicopter crash when a slow death by starvation at my own hand beckoned!

Opposite top: *The* Aurora Australis *at anchor off Davis Base;*
opposite centre: *A strange blend of old and new;*
opposite bottom: *Davis Base: luxury compared with the plateau;*
below: *Going from ship to shore via Zodiac.*

I wondered what had been going through Mawson's mind as he approached, back in 1912. At a practical level, the never-ending ice of the cliffs of course would have presented a problem we didn't have. While we had had difficulties with the ice as we approached Davis Base, our journey from ship to shore had been by air. We had simply flown over the icy obstructions. It had been the presence of the seemingly uninterrupted ice cliffs that had caused Mawson to locate his base at a point where there was a natural break: the place he subsequently called Commonwealth Bay. He was to realise only later and with some regret that it was the windiest place at sea level in the world.

Things had gone well for Mawson and the AAE at this stage. The expedition's main goal was to investigate, as far as possible, the stretch of essentially unknown Antarctic coast extending between the points reached by the Terra Nova Expedition to the west and the Gauss Expedition to the east—a huge blank on the world map at that time. By January 1912 Mawson had established a base on the subantarctic Macquarie Island, building a telegraph station there, and had sent a party west under the leadership of Frank Wild to establish a small base on the Shackleton ice shelf. The remainder of the summer at Commonwealth Bay had involved setting up the base, building a hut and catching seal and penguin meat for the dogs; most of these tasks had been completed successfully.

Mawson was probably full of hope and excited anticipation at the heady prospect of what he was about to discover both geographically and scientifically. The following summer he would personally undertake the most eastern of the exploratory sledge expeditions, the infamous Far Eastern Sledging Party journey, expecting it to be the most dangerous of the lot. Still, he obviously had no idea of the tragic events that were to unfold for him in the process. I wondered which was worse: not knowing and having events just happen to you and then reacting to them, or deliberately disadvantaging yourself as we were doing, as a premeditated act, and hoping that we could handle what was coming.

We were here to deprive ourselves—deliberately—of sufficient food, adequate shelter and modern equipment in a bid to scrutinise events that befell Mawson on the same trip. For us at

Opposite top: *A helicopter 'slinging' equipment ashore. Helicopters are the workhorses of the Antarctic;*
opposite bottom: *The helicopters were flown by highly experienced pilots Frank, Dave and Rick.*

this stage, the same terrible conditions that Mawson had faced lay only a few days away, and more than once I wished for some last-minute problem to delay us just a bit longer to allow me time to better prepare myself. At that moment I would have taken *The Matrix*'s blue pill and happily not known. Ignorance can, after all, be bliss.

The ice extended to the horizon in all directions as we homed in on the small collection of makeshift buildings that constituted the Skiway. There, next to them, was a pile of equipment under netting: the old sled, boxes and tent cover that we would use for our attempt. It looked an insignificant and pretty rickety assemblage of old gear, woefully inadequate for the task ahead. Best not to think about it too much now. After a hasty check to make sure everything was accounted for, cold forced us to retreat into the freezer container of the hut for a quick meal, then bed. It was Boxing Day, but it didn't feel like it.

I climbed into the reindeer-skin sleeping bag for the first time, thinking it wise to start turning back the clock and getting familiar with the old equipment immediately, knowing that this gear would have to sustain us in the harshest of places in just a few days' time. The bag was curiously comforting; quite literally it was like climbing inside the hollowed-out inverted carcass of an animal, the long hairs soft against your skin. It was musty and mildly claustrophobic, but it felt warm here inside the hut at 5°C at least; how it would cope at −20°C remained to be seen.

I felt satisfied that the team and apparently all of the equipment were here intact, but in my mind I felt a real sense of disquiet. It was more than just what lay ahead. Mostly it related to how well I felt that we would gel as a team more generally. There had been tensions on ship—inevitable when you put a group of six chiefs together with no Indians. I just hoped that Antarctica with all of the challenges it presented would pull us together rather than cause more tension. As a group we all had our niches and on paper were a formidable team. John and I had already formed a close bond. I was the more experienced polar traveller, but John was the better climber, and we mutually respected one another's abilities. It wasn't

Previous page: *Ephemeral, icy worlds stretching into the distance;*
opposite: *The fractured tumult of a glacier as it reaches the Antarctic coast, with crevasses routinely 100 metres deep.*

our relationship that I was worried about but rather how well he and I would interact with the film crew, knowing the importance of our focusing on the task at hand with the minimum of disruption.

It had not of course always been smooth sailing within the AAE. Mawson was seen by several of the party to be somewhat harsh and aloof, someone who imposed his will on others and who did not always see eye to eye with the ship's captain, John King Davis, and stronger personalities such as Frank Hurley. Their radio operator too had suffered something of a mental breakdown and had been confined to quarters: part of Mawson's draconian measure to control him.

Thankfully, the dynamic of our team was nothing like that, but it was inevitable that there would be some personality tensions. It brought into clear focus for me the fact that I will happily accommodate others' idiosyncrasies if I feel that they are pulling in the same direction as me. If not, I tend to lose interest and switch off from them, being particularly sensitive when it comes to polar journeys. If I have to exert my authority over others to the detriment of truly experiencing a place like Antarctica, it flies in the face of the reasons I go there. I didn't want to have to impose my will on anyone and felt that with John there would be no need for it. He and I got on well and were both single-minded about what needed to happen for success in this trip. The film crew could take care of themselves. I just hoped they wouldn't be a distraction out on the ice.

The weather wasn't promising. Overnight a strong wind of 55 kilometres an hour had picked up, bringing with it poor visibility and difficult conditions in which to load the sled. It reminded me of the difficulty of doing things in this place. We packed as best we could and tried to erect the 'tent', such as it was. But it was too windy and after several attempts, grappling with madly flapping canvas, we retreated into the hut to sit out the storm.

The following morning, the wind was light and we set about organising the gear again in earnest.

Mawson and his two colleagues were at the easternmost point of their journey when tragedy struck. Ninnis, his entire dog team and the sled they pulled fell through a snow bridge that Mawson, in charge of the first sled, and Mertz, travelling on skis, had managed to cross safely just moments before.

> *We sounded to the ledge with a furlong line—150 feet [46 m] sheer, ice ledge. No sign of Ninnis—must have struck it & been killed instantly then gone on down. Our ropes not long enough to go down, or the sledge to span the crevasse.*

Mawson's account continued:

> *Practically all food had gone down, spade, pick, tent, Mertz's burberry trousers & helmet, cup, spoons, mast, sail etc. We had our sleeping bags, a week and a half food, the spare tent without poles, & our private bags & cooker & kerosene. The dogs in my team were very poorly & the worst, & no feed for them—the other team comprised the picked dogs, all dog food, & almost all man food. We considered it a possibility to get through to Winter Quarters by eating dogs, so 9 hours after the accident started back, but terribly handicapped.*

The loss of Ninnis effectively sealed the fate of Mawson and Mertz by leaving them with little chance of surviving the return journey to the Winter Quarters hut with the meagre amounts of food and equipment left to them. It was Day 34 of the outward journey for the party on what to date had been a successful expedition, the dogs pulling the provisions and the men alternating between riding on the sleds or walking or running alongside. Suddenly the chances of the two men surviving looked bleak.

We were starting our journey from the point where the original expedition went wrong. We would be spared Mawson and Mertz's outward journey, but we were less fit, less acclimatised to the cold, and would have no dogs to help us either pull the sled or provide a walking source of food, as Mawson and Mertz had had for the first two weeks of their survival bid. With the exception of the dogs, which are no longer permitted in Antarctica for environmental reasons, we dutifully kept to the exact specification of what Mawson had with him after the accident, and now laid it out on the snow in front of us. It was a pitiful sight.

It was the first time all of the gear had been together in one place, and it didn't look remotely sufficient for what we were about to attempt. We were left with a 'tent' with no floor, meaning we would have to sleep on the snow and likely get extremely wet and cold as a result. The poles to hold the old tent cover up were a pair of heavy wooden skis and a pair of sled runners, and there were no guy lines, pegs or spares of anything. Any modifications to the equipment we made only with tools and materials that Mawson would have had available to him— a knife, hand drill, needle and a couple of thicknesses of twine. Our guy lines were made from unravelling thicker rope and attaching it to the walls of the tent by looping it around bunched-up clumps of fabric. Pegs were rough hewn with a knife from offcuts from the old sled runners. John, like Mertz before him, had no overtrousers. Our food for the whole expedition filled only half a small box and consisted mainly of congealed lard, small amounts of sugar and a few dozen sledge biscuits.

Expeditions are, to a large extent, about self-delusion and keeping your emotions in check. You convince yourself that things are going well, that you are on track, that all will be fine, that you are in good shape, all in the face of evidence completely to the contrary. In my opinion, these are prerequisite skills for conducting expeditions. But with the motley collection of equipment and food laid out before us, it was difficult to feel too positive about things.

As the camera rolled, the angst on John's face and mine was real.

2 The Plateau

The project to retrace Mawson's steps was an unusual beast and an extremely complex logistical exercise—much as expeditions back in the heroic era had been. It was a real-life expedition about which a film was being made and, as such, was funded almost entirely by film money and considerable logistical in-kind support from the Australian Antarctic Division.

This resulted in some interesting situations, to say the least, particularly with some items of our gear. For reasons of process, larger items—such as the sled—had to be acquired through Film Australia's procurement channels. Furthermore, some items were delivered straight to the wharves for passage to Antarctica ahead of the team, which travelled on another vessel. This, combined with the geographic spread of the team in Melbourne, Adelaide, Sydney and Hobart, meant that neither I nor John saw several items of gear before they were sent to Antarctica, and saw other items only when we arrived in Hobart a few days ahead of our sailing date. This left little time for adjustment if something was not right, which was not good when we would rely on this gear for our survival.

Previous page: *John and me in harness, working like the dogs we replaced.*

Now that John and I had finally gone through all the equipment, a few things were brought into sharp perspective for us. The gear I had sourced for my unsupported polar expedition, with tough conditions in mind, differed dramatically in quality from some of the poor equipment supplied for this trip. A number of items were no more than props or were seriously lacking in some way, in particular the main expedition boxes, which were made of thin walled wood with long screws protruding several centimetres inside them. They looked fine from the outside but could have been specifically designed to rupture fuel containers, stoves and food bags. Furthermore, the calico bags and aluminium pot we had ordered had not materialised; as for the stove, it struggled to retain pressure, which meant that its burners didn't work properly. Luckily, I had brought a reliable old spare primus of my own and a large aluminium pot just in case.

My boots were another example. I had managed at the eleventh hour to get hobnails fitted onto them in Tasmania, having had the chance to check the ones supplied for me before boarding ship. The boots had had no hobnails on the soles, meaning that they would have had no grip whatsoever on the snow.

Above: *Hooking up the crew's equipment to a snowmobile, the modern version of a dog team;* opposite: *The last call before turning the clock back 100 years.*

But these fortunate breaks weren't the point. We felt badly let down by the suppliers, who had endangered us and our expedition with substandard equipment. I was irritated, as it suggested to me how little people cared for the functionality of our gear and, in effect, for our well-being. John was furious. For him, and Russians generally, loyalty is very important. Supplying substandard equipment that could directly impact on our ability to function or survive represented a personal affront to him, not to mention the hassle of having to deal with the problems caused by thoughtlessness. It added to our feeling that having film involvement with something as serious as a polar man-haul expedition might mean compromising our chances of success, and that the goals of the film-makers were not the same as ours. Real or imagined, it was not the last time I was to have such thoughts.

We were going into one of the most inhospitable environments on Earth with starvation rations and a skeleton selection of equipment replicating gear from a century before. Our summer weather window was also closing fast; we were already a week behind where Mawson's expedition had been at the same time. This was nobody's fault; it was simply due to the timing of our passage south. I knew the number of blizzard days in February in Antarctica to be far greater than in January and that we would also start to experience some darkness and much colder temperatures as nights drew in. We needed to be under way.

Above: *Antarctica: not an easy place for humans to survive.*

By late evening on 29 December, tempers were well and truly frayed. John and I had spent the day poring over gear, repairing items damaged in transit, filing down screws, cleaning and testing the stove and drilling holes in the sled runners that would form part of our tent. It was sedentary work and the cold had seeped into our bones, but I was determined to get going that night. In the final analysis, there is no real way to ease into a polar trip. There comes a point where you go from a position of warmth and relative safety to one where your life depends on your wits and what you pull behind you in your sled. It is the point at which you switch into survival mode, the cold forcing you into continuous movement to generate heat.

My obsession with getting moving sat uneasily with John's quest for perfection. John wanted to check things, have a decent night's rest and set off the next day having made one final check. But perfection was one word that didn't feature in this journey, except when it came to our daily food intake calculations. We were starting from a point of deliberate disadvantage, the same disadvantage faced by Mawson following the loss of Ninnis. Leaving with a partial collection of old equipment for such a momentous task felt alien to me too, but that was the nature of this trip. Staying another night served no good purpose anyway. It meant unloading the sled, tying everything down, getting the sleeping bags out and spending another fraught night. The mood around the Skiway was beginning to get to me, and the weather now was, relatively speaking, good. At midnight, after an hour of filming, we moved off, desperately cold, stiff and tired, but glad at least to have started.

With our first steps we were turning what had always been a future event into a reality; the idea of emulating Mawson was now an actual test of survival for us, with the fundamental difference that ours was a voluntary exercise while Mawson's had been a journey of necessity. Even so, our expedition could have serious consequences if things went wrong, and it was imperative to start focusing on the task of staying alive in Antarctica, regardless of the original motive for the journey.

The sled creaked into life as we leaned into the harnesses for the first time. We weren't pulling in time and were moving into a headwind, but nevertheless getting going was something of a relief. The sled scudded across the cold wind-pack and the frustration of the previous days fell away. It soon returned. The solid-packed snow around the Skiway, the result of grooming, soon gave way to hard, rutted sastrugi (a landscape of wave-shaped snow and ice carved by the wind that ravages Antarctica) and then rutted blue ice within 200 metres. The sled began snagging under the lips of standing waves of sastrugi, some 30 centimetres high, that stood up defiantly in front of us. Every 20 metres or so, a big piece of sastrugi stopped the sled dead. Trying to pull it through required a synchronised effort by John and me much like the timing required to get the best out of a rowing crew. Pulling separately and out of time was no good.

John's old army boots had a rubberised tread, with the result that he skittered around on the ice, falling heavily several times. My hobnails, with studs like those of a golf shoe, at least cut into the ice reasonably well, but, without John's power, I struggled to get the sled over the sastrugi on my own. We battled on for twenty minutes, both unsure whether the conditions were going to remain like this and, if so, how to overcome them. Between heavy breaths, I suggested to John that the icy sastrugi were due to the fact that the katabatic (downhill) winds here were stronger, as we were climbing quite steeply. The steeper the slope in Antarctica, the harder the wind, as it pours downhill like water, stripping the snow away and leaving just ice underfoot. John grunted in acknowledgement. Understanding the reasons behind our predicament didn't make things any easier.

Previous page: *Moving off on a bitterly cold, windy day, wearing Burberry hoods to prevent frostbite to the ears;* opposite: *Wearing my finneskos, boots made of reindeer skin.*

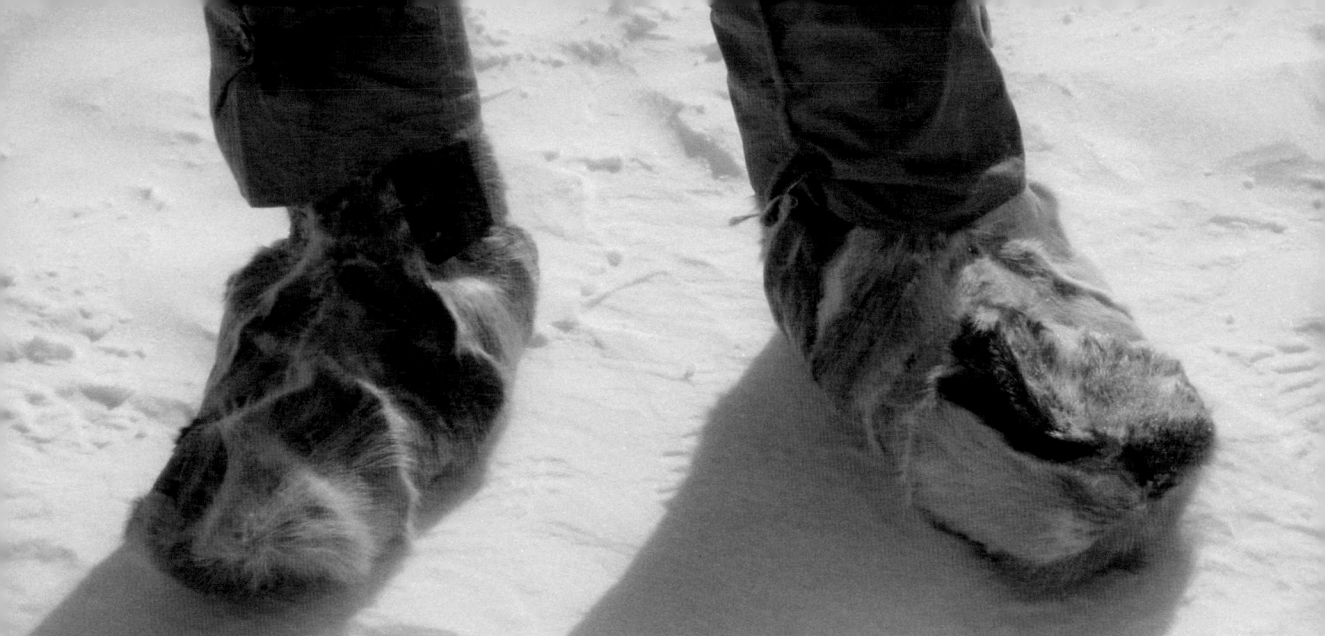

The first hour was interminable. We stopped and had the second of our meagre ration of five boiled sweets each for the day. It had been difficult to warm up and John was lucky not to have suffered injury from his frequent acrobatic falls. The sled's length and flexibility meant that it bent and contorted, hugging the contours of the ground and maximising drag. The headwind was stiffening, the hill steepened and it was getting colder too. We had travelled less than 2 kilometres.

Two hours of slog later it was 3 a.m., and a large red sun sat just above the horizon. Completely exhausted, we stopped, stepping out of the harnesses to put up the tent for the first time. It was not a tent so much as a collection of a tent's component parts with many of the critical bits missing—Mawson described it in his diary as 'a crude tent devised by draping the remaining tent cover over skis and sledge struts', the rest having fallen down the crevasse with Ninnis and his dog team.

While John chipped away at the icy ground with the spade to make holes in which to plant our improvised tent poles, I untied the ropes that secured the tent to the sled. They had come loose anyway and I made a mental note to do something about them later. We certainly could not afford to lose anything. The 'tent' weighed about 20 kilograms and the skis and sled runners of the improvised frame were completely disproportionate to the flimsy tent cover that we slung over them and crudely stitched into place with some twine. As was the case with Mawson's tent, the cover had no guy lines or floor sheet, with the pegs being ones we had fashioned the day before

with the knife from offcuts from the sled runners. John climbed inside the tent and extended the legs of the frame into the holes he had carved, as I dug a series of snow blocks from an area of drifted snow nearby, heaving them onto the skirt of the tent to weigh it down. It was important to get this right. The tent cover, together with its motley collection of supports, would need to be bombproof when the inevitable gale-force winds came to visit.

I followed John inside, wriggling through the tunnel of fabric that formed the tent entrance, and tied it shut behind me with twine, glad to be out of the wind. We had to act quickly to keep our bodies and our sleeping bags as far away from the snow as possible—a difficult feat when lying on the ground with no groundsheet.

In a sleeping bag, most heat is lost through the ground regardless of the surface you are on. Lying on snow is to be avoided at all costs. The flipside of cold air getting into your sleeping bag is that your body heat escapes and warms up the ground beneath you. If this is snow—as it was in our case—the escaping body heat melts it, making your sleeping bag wet. This can be disastrous, as, quite apart from the fact that you are cold already, you have very little opportunity to dry yourself. To compound things further, this wetness will freeze as soon as you take your body heat out of the equation, as happens when you put the sleeping bag on the sled. There, your sleeping bag will remain frozen until you unroll it and your body heat melts it again, and so you become wetter and wetter. Your bag rapidly loses much of its capacity to keep you warm—hence the need for swift action to avoid it happening.

We quickly removed layers: beaver-pelt mitts, woollen gloves, finneskos (reindeer-skin boots), balaclavas and our Burberry jackets were laid out on the floor beneath us in as even a layer as possible, and the sleeping bags placed on top. Everything we had we put beneath us, even the Australian and Union Jack flags—anything to insulate us from the ground below, regardless of how heinous a crime it probably was to place your feet on your country's colours. Almost an hour had passed since we stopped. It was 4 a.m. and I was seriously cold, my hands shaking and teeth chattering. I don't normally feel the cold too badly, and it showed me that I had been running on empty for a while, what with the stress of getting under way, the cold and

Opposite top: *Two men adrift on a frozen sea;*
opposite bottom: *Like creases in a sheet: crevasses viewed from the air.*

the expectation. We killed the primus just before 5 a.m. (not that it made much difference to the temperature in the tent) and lay in silence. There was no doubt this was going to be an extremely tough trip. With sensation slowly returning to my feet I drifted into an uneasy sleep, the weak sun still up.

Mawson's thoughts on the first day of his return trek were of great sadness at the loss of 'our loved companion Ninnis' yet, in typical fashion, he focused on the immediate task at hand, which was getting back to the cache of food they had left 40 kilometres behind them the previous night before the wind obscured their tracks. Five and a half hours after leaving Ninnis in his icy grave they had reached it, and their mood was as good as could be expected, given all that had happened. It was testament to Mawson's ability to compartmentalise experiences and emotions and then move on—one that led to accusations by some of a coldness and lack of compassion. In my view his skill of treating good and bad incidents alike went with the territory of polar trips and was an approach with which I could identify. As Kipling said: 'if you can meet with triumph and disaster and treat those two impostors just the same'.

John and I meanwhile needed momentum, but we felt like we were moving backwards, so we were in quite a different place psychologically from Mawson and Mertz. They would have been relieved to have covered the ground and made it to the extra food cache. With their dogs assisting them they covered the same distance in an hour that we had taken all night to do—a paltry 9 kilometres.

I woke to the sensation of the windward side of the tent pressing against my head. It was 1 p.m. and outside was a cauldron of swirling drift. I lay there not wanting to get out of the bag. 'Russky!' I shouted, eliciting a slow stirring in the adjacent sleeping bag in response. Leaning on one arm, I put on my sweater and Burberry and tried to work out what the day might hold for us, as John lit the stove, injecting a couple of loads of meths into the burner before it was finally warm enough to light the more stubborn kerosene as the flame turned from an orange glow to an intense blue. I had no idea what temperature it was in the tent, but the snow all around us made it feel miserably cold and grey.

Previous page: *Sorting gear on a rare day without wind;*
opposite, clockwise from top left: *John and me making running repairs; walking into a headwind, risking frostbite to our faces; smiles for the camera; sorting the gear; John fixing unravelling rope with twine on a still day.*

Five blocks of snow from the floor of our home produced enough water to drink and to boil up our first 'hoosh'—the name given by the early explorers to a mixed broth of everything they had. In our case it wasn't much: a block about the size of a mobile phone of congealed lard mixed with ground-up beef jerky known as 'pemmican', to which we added two-thirds of a whey biscuit broken into pieces and some ground-up dog-meat substitute. We had chosen kangaroo jerky, as its leanness is very close to that of dog meat. On polar trips lean is bad, as fat is what is needed for energy. The resultant mix was acrid, oily, bitter and incredibly unpleasant-tasting—even worse than its unpromising individual ingredients, if that were possible. It made me retch. John was apparently something of a lard connoisseur, shaking his head disapprovingly and claiming that it was of poor quality. We washed it all down with a mug of weak tea fortified by a small amount of sugar, then rolled up the bags, revealing patches of wet where our makeshift 'mattresses' had failed to insulate us from the snow and ice below. This did not bode well: it meant they had not served their purpose and that the inexorable process of moisture accumulation had begun. It was a miserable place in which we found ourselves. We cajoled our boots onto sore feet; the previously pliable leather had been transformed by frozen sweat into something resembling wood, which gradually thawed with the warmth from our feet.

Above: *Pemmican's two constituents: kangaroo jerky (left) and lard (right). Truly revolting when combined.*

It was scant consolation, but I knew Mawson's lot had been even worse than ours. He had had to dispatch his loyal canine companions, knowing that the only way they would make it was to feed the dogs to one another, supplementing the dogs' food with worn-out finneskos, mitts and rawhide straps—basically anything they might be able to digest. In keeping with this, the weakest dog, George, was killed after their first day's travel, on 15 December, and was fed to the other five, with Mawson and Mertz also frying up some of him for their breakfast. 'Although the meat was tough and stringy, every scrap was eaten, including the paws which were stewed', Mawson wrote.

We left at 6 p.m., having taken more than four hours to melt water and break camp, and found ourselves climbing again almost immediately. Going uphill in stiff boots was hard on the heels. At least, I hoped we were going uphill. If not, we were slower than I thought possible. My mood fluctuated between thinking I wasn't up to the task and reminding myself logically that this must be a steep section of climbing and that we weren't yet expedition fit. I just hoped we would enjoy a period of improved fitness in a few days' time, before lack of food inevitably dragged us down through loss of weight and strength.

The air temperature at this time of day was cold, as the sun sat low above the horizon, imparting little warmth. Although this made the snow colder and firmer to walk on, the benefit was outweighed by the fact that the sled did not want to glide. I had experienced this before on polar trips but this time it seemed far worse, the wooden runners of the sled being wide and designed for a far heavier load than we had on board. Spreading the weight over a larger surface area meant that the sled was too light to exert the pressure needed to melt the snow and achieve the glide necessary for the sled to run. I hadn't the time, energy or inclination to distract myself and instead allowed the frustration to build up within me in order to derive some strength to pull this most reluctant of objects, swearing to myself as I went. My anger was not aimed at anyone in particular; instead, I berated myself for any defeatist thoughts I had had and focused my anger on the sled's reluctance to move.

Travel at night was how Mawson had also done things, for two reasons. First, Ninnis had died in the late afternoon on 14 December, thus dictating the time that Mawson and Mertz began their return journey. Second, and more significantly, Mawson felt that night-time travel with the sun lower in the sky meant colder, firmer and less energy-sapping snow conditions.

Our experience was proving very different from Mawson's. His diary describes his second day's travel as 'good and hard and comparatively smooth. Halted at 18.5 miles [30 km]'. In contrast, at the end of an exhausting day where we had thrown everything into the task, by midnight we had managed a measly 10 kilometres. I decided that only when we started gaining on Mawson's daily averages could we afford some direct comparison between our distances and his. Until then it was counter-productive. He still had dogs pulling along with him and it showed.

Day 3 began much as the previous day had done, the slope seemingly rising up to meet us as we edged towards a horizon that seemed very close. The wind had dropped and the conditions became cloudy, leaving us hot and sweating in less than half an hour in a balmy −10°C. We removed the Burberry jackets to work in our thermals and jumpers, and stepped back into the harnesses, keen to cover ground.

After a couple of hours of intense effort we sat on the sled to rest, clumsily unwrapping a boiled sweet each with mitted hands, resting until the cold forced us to get moving again a few short minutes later. This was a landscape of uneven sastrugi, startlingly white to the horizon, with no sign of life anywhere now that we were 40 kilometres inland and 1000 metres high. The wind began to pick up, making us reach for our Burberrys again for warmth. I untied the arms of my jacket from around the mast of the sled, but John's was not where he had left it, wedged tight under the spade. It became clear almost immediately that as we had moved over the rough sastrugi the jacket had shaken loose and had been left behind somewhere. Our minds raced. It was a potential disaster: the Burberrys were our only windproof layer in an already meagre assembly of clothing. John had already started at a disadvantage, wearing only woollen undertrousers to replicate Mertz's situation, as he had lost his when Ninnis fell into the crevasse. Now John had no top layer either. It would be the beginning of the end for him and our partnership early in the piece if we could not recover his jacket.

We had to think quickly. To retrieve the jacket—if it had not been lost or blown away already—we obviously had to retrace our steps. That was harder and more dangerous than you might think, given that the jacket might be 4 or 5 kilometres behind us. It would be a

Opposite: *A good flat section made the going a little easier.*

huge effort there and back with the sled, and we would be quicker without it. If John went back alone, he stood the chance of losing me and the sled, as the ground was still icy enough to make tracks difficult to see. If we went together, we could lose the sled completely as the strengthening wind could reduce visibility in minutes. A lot could happen in the hours it might take either one of us to backtrack and return. Even if John were to take our only compass, things could still go wrong, as our route had meandered through sastrugi large enough for the jacket to be only metres from our track yet remain hidden. We decided the best option was to leave the sled behind and for John to go back alone, trying to follow our outward tracks. I would then follow his tracks, making the trail clearer and easier to follow back to the sled. If I kept a distance behind him, I could keep both him and the sled in sight for as long as possible, and provide him with a point of reference when he turned around.

I walked along some distance behind John, the ease of walking downhill without the sled giving me space to think of the dire consequences to our trip if he could not find his jacket. Its loss was not scripted and the options were bleak. Either we would have to fashion a new jacket (and if so, from what?), or we would have to share the one we had (totally impractical), or, the least palatable option of all, either John or I would have to drop out, the other going on alone at this early stage in the trip.

I wasn't angered by the jacket loss as much as I was concerned with finding it. John was annoyed enough with himself for both of us anyway, and had sworn copiously in Russian before storming off back towards the coast to find it. Our roles of a few days previously had swiftly reversed: I now urged caution while he was all for rushing off to recover both his jacket and the situation as quickly as possible. I looked up for a moment and in the distance saw a figure waving his arms, almost imperceptibly getting larger as he slowly approached. He had found the jacket and disaster had been averted.

Reunited, I was surprised at how philosophically I took it. In all honesty, I was just relieved and I knew how John felt about it. He was a resourceful man with great reserves of patience and that meant he normally did things right, so I knew how galling such a serious oversight must have been for him. We did not need any hot-headedness from me, or to keep a running ledger of who had done what, right or wrong, for the rest of the trip. That wasn't really my style; nor was it John's. If I am honest, part of me did secretly regard it as something of a credit in the bank of our personal relationship, which might help to diffuse a situation in the future if roles were reversed. John had a tendency to get irritated with the inefficiency of others, including mine, some of it justified, some of it less so. His hatred of waste and inexactitude meant that he would pore over situations for far longer than me. Between us we made a good team.

Positives, at least, could be derived from the jacket situation. It had been a careless mistake, but the way we had reacted, overcoming it as a team, was very positive. Regarding it as a false start, we pushed off afresh as if it were the beginning of our day's travel. My philosophical

mood from the initial loss of the jacket through to our safe return to the sled almost two and a half hours later was something of a record for me, but I knew it wouldn't last forever. Sure enough, it had completely evaporated after less than half an hour of toil amongst the sastrugi.

When we stopped I wrote in my diary entry: 'The sled pulls very, very poorly, and feels desperately heavy'. Unfortunately, this was rapidly becoming the default position. With self-preservation in mind, I began to adjust my mindset away from the relentless pursuit of kilometres and daily averages to the far more realistic proposition of just doing what we could, like Mawson. His goal went from making it back to base to simply getting as far as he could with an increasing belief that Providence would determine how far that would be. It was surprising how thinking this way lifted the pressure and, with the addition of a few drops of raw alcohol into our tea that night, the mood picked up considerably. John lit a candle (not for effect but to raise the temperature in the tent by a few degrees) and talked of the old days, growing up on a farm in Siberia. He could really string out his stories, so that midway through his getting lost as a child hunting for berries in the Taiga forests, I found myself drifting off to sleep. It was New Year's Eve.

Above: *The tent, relatively hole-free at this early stage of the expedition, in the midst of this austere but beautiful place.*

3 Stopka

It was half-past two in the afternoon on 2 January—our fifth day—but we were not going anywhere. We were completely blizzard-bound, with visibility of only a couple of metres and the wind howling around us, looking for a way into our small sanctuary. Five days of subjecting the tent to Antarctic conditions meant that there were now plenty of opportunities for the wind to get in, mainly via a dozen or so holes of varying size. Cold air and spindrift poured in. The valances, too, haemorrhaged heat as the wind found ways to get in between the snow blocks that weighed them down.

. . .

It had been no oil painting to start with, but the tent was now massively distorted due to huge pressure on the windward side and a strange vacuum on the leeward side that sucked the fabric outwards.

'*Stopka*', sighed John deeply as he squinted through a narrow opening in the door of the tent. I agreed, getting a rough idea of what he had said. *Stopka* seemed to be a Russian term for an enforced rest, and it certainly fitted the bill. John had such a repertoire of words and

Previous page: *The blizzard line running from the crew's tent to ours ensured that on this occasion they could find us.*

expressions borrowed from various languages, and his delivery was so deadpan that statements, questions, jokes and criticism were often interchangeable, making reaction to them tricky. Often I would respond to a statement when no response was required or remain silent after what had been a cunningly disguised joke. He was a great character, of that there was no doubt, and I felt this whole experience was the better for his being there. *Stopka* certainly summed up where we were.

As the day moved ponderously along, it became difficult to keep the mood up. We both agreed that periods of enforced inactivity were the worst aspect of expeditions, something I felt particularly strongly. I like to keep moving every day, getting through the task at hand and not hanging around. Stopping took a lot of patience, and I found it far more mentally draining than moving. On my first polar foray, when I experienced such stoppages I tended to lack confidence, worrying that delays would mean I would be unable to regain my momentum.

Previous page: *The spade being used as an anchor, attached with a rope to the top of the tent;*
above left: *An old 'Polar Pyramid': Mawson's tent would have looked similar to this one before the loss of Ninnis;*
above right: *Some things never change. A modern 'Polar Pyramid' tent—the same basic design as 100 years before.*

With experience and soul-searching over the course of other journeys, I have now built up a certain resilience, knowing that, from somewhere, the resolve to keep going seems to emerge. But delays still affect me and I always wonder if there will be a time when I find myself being physically and mentally unable to continue.

The critical extra pressure on this trip was that the longer we spent motionless, the more valuable food we used up and the longer our odds became of making it. Already we were way behind Mawson and Mertz, having travelled only 42 kilometres to their 120. Our progress had been unconvincing. On Day 1 we had started late at night, thinking the snow would be firmer, but the temperature was so cold that it had made going extremely hard. On Day 2 we had slogged away, climbing into a headwind all day, and it was again desperately hard work. On Day 3 the weather was greatly improved but John's jacket cost us two hours of wasted backtracking, effort and stress. Day 4 was probably the best day we had had, although it was the day on which we discovered a major tear in the tent, casting serious doubts on its ability to survive the conditions even if we ourselves fared reasonably well. And so to Day 5: tent-bound in a blizzard. I drifted into slumber—the best way to handle things.

I woke a couple of hours later, the wind still roaring around the tent. I got the stove going, boiled up a weak brew, reusing, as Mawson did, my one tea bag for the day, and ate a sweet. I was incredibly hungry but we had already had our hoosh, deciding to eat our normal ration while tent-bound to try to keep our strength up for when the weather broke. I attempted to look at things philosophically, convincing myself that these conditions were what Mawson and Mertz had endured and that I wanted to be as close as possible to their experience, in order to understand what they had gone through. I flicked through Mawson's diary to gain some insight into how he had felt at the same point. It was consoling to read that Mawson and Mertz had experienced similar conditions. But, typical of the man who wrote them, Mawson's words themselves did not give me any great insight into how he was actually feeling. His diary entries are strangely detached and concerned mainly with the logistics of how the two men were travelling.

I had not thought about it much before the trip, but I suppose I had assumed that our timeline would roughly mirror Mawson and Mertz's—we would go well initially and then slow, as they did, as we weakened and experienced more inclement weather towards February and the end of summer. At this stage, though, things were very different. Mawson and Mertz had achieved great distances early on and slowed later. We, on the other hand, had been slow from the outset, and early problems with the tent and lack of food were already affecting our strength and ability to keep warm. It didn't bode well.

As if being stuck wasn't enough, the tent was getting worse. Another large rip had appeared when a massive gust of wind bowed the tent inwards, causing the fabric to tear on the metal edge of the food box we brought in each night. John had worked hard to fix it with fine twine, hoping it would not tear further, but the ease with which it ripped was a real worry.

The multiple smaller holes meant that the temperature in the tent stayed low, although at least they provided views of the outside world. All was a swirling mass of sprindrift. It was utterly inhospitable. The sled, half buried, was just visible 5 or so metres away, held in place by a couple of strategically positioned ice axes. We had a small wind-speed meter, not as a concession to modernity but to record conditions for comparison with Mawson's journey. It recorded a wind speed of about 80 kilometres an hour when held at arm's length from the tent. Looking out at the scene, I figured that anything more than 50 to 60 kilometres an hour would be too much for us to travel in. I went to sleep with the wind showing no signs of abating. It had been blowing hard now for almost fifteen hours.

Waking several hours later, the noise inside the tent was louder than ever as the ill-fitting cover flapped furiously against the tent frame, the wind roaring with an even greater intensity than before. I was not too worried about the pyramid frame of the tent. What worried me was the questionable strength of the tent fabric. John and I looked at one another, wondering if it would hold.

With a steadily strengthening wind, by early afternoon we reckoned we were already at the limits of what this tent could be expected to handle. I didn't dare open the door to survey the scene properly, despite its position on the leeward side of the tent, for fear of placing some extra stress on the structure or being inundated with drift. Judging by the buffeting we were receiving, we were sure the wind must have increased to more than 100 kilometres per hour. The atmosphere was tense as we both sensed impending structural failure. The only thing to do was to pack all of our possessions into the food box, put on all of our clothes and put all of our essentials into our sleeping bags with us. If worst came to worst and the tent blew away, we would just have to let the snow drift over us, try to survive in the sleeping bags in the drift and, with luck, reassess later: not much of a plan but the best we could come up with. What it meant for the expedition was obviously serious but not as serious as the immediate threat of lying open to the elements with no shelter.

We sat half in our sleeping bags with our heads and shoulders propped against the tent's windward side to take some pressure off the fabric, staring incredulously at the funnel of material that was normally the door being sucked outwards like a windsock or as if someone were frantically tugging on it, trying to get in.

We drifted in and out of sleep, finally giving up at about five in the afternoon in order to light the stove. The sun was up there somewhere, and the temperature in the tent a relatively warm −5°C, with the temperature outside probably 4 or 5 degrees colder. The wind was still ferocious and visibility was only a few metres, meaning there remained no chance of travel. You can never afford to take Antarctica lightly—if it wants to get rid of you it can do so very easily. In our case, if the wind speed rose much higher, the tent wouldn't hold. It did not matter how close the film crew were to us if that happened: if they were more than a few hundred metres away with visibility of no more than a couple of metres, both of which were relatively common occurrences, we would not find them. Neither that scenario nor the crew's enjoyment of modern equipment, warm clothes and plentiful food were worth thinking about.

Given that it was our second full day in the tent, we decided to have only a half ration in a bid to save food. The 'meal' was pitiful: half a biscuit in a broth of watery pemmican and a handful of kangaroo jerky, washed down with a cup of weak tea, followed by a single cube of chocolate. Considering this, we managed to remain reasonably positive, busying ourselves with repairs to clothes, routine maintenance to the stove and calculating weight reduction strategies for our equipment. It was too windy to risk trying to fix holes in the tent for fear it would tear further, given the tautness of the fabric.

During this period of inaction and worry, we both handled the conditions in our own way. For John this meant internalising his feelings for much of the time, focusing on the repairs and writing intensely in his tiny pocket diary, which he filled with Cyrillic script the size of microfiche. That was his way. Not one to vocalise how he was feeling, he busied himself or lay in his bag silently, in deep thought. I am not sure whether he felt that he had nothing to contribute or chose not to say anything, or whether the uncertainty of our predicament meant he was battling at some fundamental level to deal with fears and insecurities. Possibly he needed quiet time to think his way through things and overcome fears of failure or worse.

As this was the first time I had undertaken a journey with him, his extended periods of silence were difficult for me. I was convinced I had offended him. For someone like me, who likes to take situations head on and get things out in the open, I found the silence hard to handle. It made me feel the solitude far more than if I had been on my own. When I pushed him, I was given gruff assurances that there was no problem and so decided against my better judgement to leave him alone. Hours later, out of the blue, John offered me a weak tea, heralding the end of his quiet period and one in which he was happy to talk, the mood of several hours evaporating harmlessly. It was just his way and something I became accustomed to, although never truly used to.

Opposite: *John, draped in his sleeping bag, striking a 'Peter the Great' pose.*

John worked tirelessly, stitching some 'lanyards' onto our woollen mitts (strips of material attached to the gloves that went around the neck to stop them blowing away when you took them off). I kept my mind active by focusing on the two main variables of the trip: sled weight and how to reduce it, and how much time we could pull the sled for each day. I began calculating how we could combine our powdered milk and hot chocolate to free one of the tins to save weight. After an hour's calculation and decanting, a 200-gram weight-saving in the form of the empty hot chocolate tin was the outcome. It was not the weight so much as keeping the mind active and achieving little victories that was the key. We made several other decisions about things that we could lose to reduce weight: one of the ice axes, my crampons, plus a couple of pairs of spare socks. We found ourselves, as Mawson did, discarding anything that wasn't absolutely essential (the film crew picked up these items: we actually left nothing whatsoever behind). In following the pattern of Mawson's decision-making, we started to feel closer to him.

Previous page: *Stopka: not much to smile about*;
above, from left to right: *Spindrift covers my boot in no time after removing it to put on my finnesko; the tent: welcome after a hard day; spindrift, making its way into the tent from one of the many holes in the canvas; a blizzard sets in.*

As for how much time I felt we could spend pulling the sled each day, I remained sure that around five hours was all that was sustainable. We had gradually brought our day's travel forward, having noticed that travelling through the night, although good in theory, was awful in practice. There was no doubt that the snow was firmer, but the problem was that it was actually too cold to allow the sled to run properly, while the wind seemed to pick up routinely at about midnight, making it harder and more unpleasant to put the tent up when we stopped.

Food was a big issue for me, being the bigger man and on the same amount as John. I recalled Evans, the largest man on Scott's ill-fated expedition, during which each man had eaten equal rations while pulling one large sled. The thinking at the time was that, although Evans was on the same food as the smaller men, he would be working proportionately less hard and that somehow this would balance things out. It had not held true and he had died first. Now I was also subject to the same flawed logic.

Interestingly, there were differences in the dynamics of food consumption on our journey and Mawson's. We had calculated our food by deciding what Mawson had had available to him after Ninnis' death and dividing this amount by the forty-seven days of travel that Mawson had undertaken before he reached supplementary food. Mawson consumed his food more on the basis of his individual day's efforts and certainly did not divide it equally over the course of the trip. Much of this stemmed from the fact that Mawson could not have anticipated the bad weather and problems with Mertz that would slow down his progress in the trip's latter stages, and so ate food in slightly greater quantities earlier on until he realised what was happening and adjusted accordingly. We planned on an even consumption of the food and an even exertion of effort over the whole trip, based on what was available and what we thought was achievable. I took some solace from the fact that our slow progress over the ice may have been at least partly due to the fact that we had been eating less than Mawson in these initial stages.

Mawson and Mertz really had travelled well relative to us over the same period. A couple of things were beginning to crystallise in my mind. Mawson and Mertz were together for about 320 kilometres of the almost 500 kilometres that Mawson covered. For the first 270 kilometres, they had dogs, with the faithful Ginger shot on Day 14 and consumed shortly thereafter. Conventional wisdom was that the dogs did very little after the mad rush to get back to the cached sled on the first day of Mawson and Mertz's return—a frantic journey that left the dogs completely spent. Much of this theory is based on Mawson's own words: he records in his diary that on Day 3, 'Johnson gave in at 5 miles [8 km] & had to be carried; Mary gave in at 9.5 m [15 km], so we had to camp. Pavlova also very much done. Bad lookout for dogs—and us'. He goes further on Day 4, writing that 'the dogs now do nothing (except Ginger). I pulled most of the load all the time—we had to put Mary in the sledge at 9.5 miles. Mertz skinned her at camp'.

Yet Mawson himself paints a slightly different picture elsewhere, stating in his diary that on Day 14, 'Ginger was still pulling' shortly before she was shot and consumed.

I was convinced it wasn't down to us as individuals. Mawson's dogs must have been making a big contribution to his progress—dogs, after all, have amazing pulling power, routinely being capable of pulling one and a half times their weight. I reserved judgement but was beginning to realise that the six dogs had played a massive part in Mawson's survival. I recorded my thoughts about our enforced incarceration in my diary:

> *Too tired to think about things any further, I went to sleep, waking at 2 p.m. on Day 7. All appeared relatively calm compared with the previous night's tumult,*

although the wind speed was still about 45 kilometres an hour. Visibility was somewhere around 100 metres. It was like the coming of spring after a long winter, and we hurried to get going while the weather held. Although John and I didn't speak, our relief was palpable.

Above: *The middle of an Antarctic 'night': bitterly cold but beautiful.*

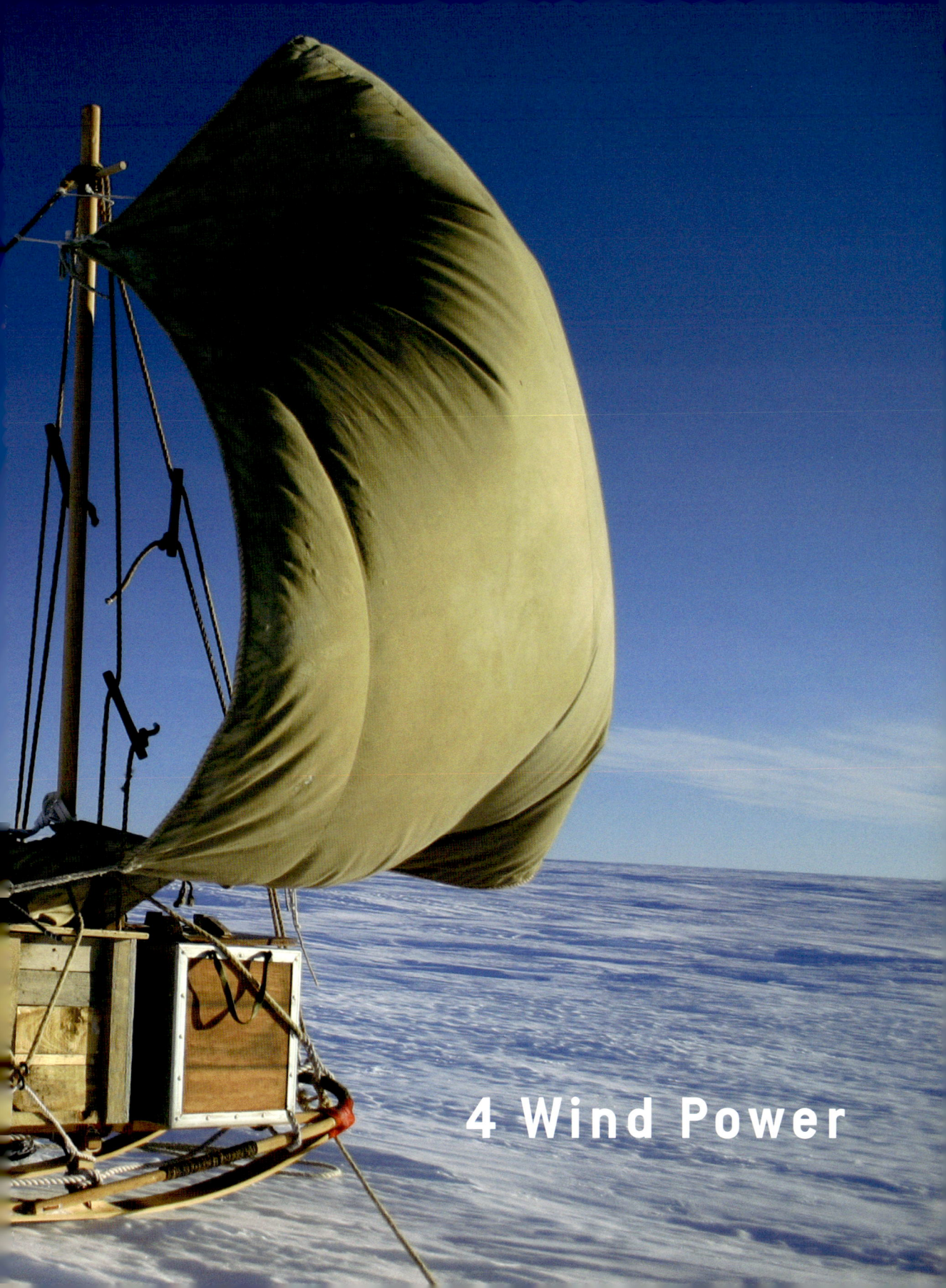

4 Wind Power

We emerged from the tent after our second day of enforced hibernation feeling sluggish and hungry rather than rested. The wind had scoured the plateau, turning the already obstructive sastrugi into a sea of angular, gnarled chop. Ironically, the tent was the one thing against which the snow could get a purchase and was by contrast heavy with accumulated snow. Jagged icicles hung off all the guy lines and ice covered the tent like icing on a Christmas cake.

. . .

Deciding to get going and actually doing it are two totally different things in Antarctica, with making and breaking camp, melting snow and mending both yourself and your equipment all taking inordinate amounts of time. By the end of our first week and with 430 kilometres still to go, we had cut the time from waking to breaking camp to about three hours, much like Mawson did. We were slowed down by routine maintenance, the time the stove took to melt snow, lack of space inside the tent, the increasing fatigue brought on by lack of food and the awkwardness of loading and tying the gear on the sled with our uncooperative heavy hemp ropes.

Previous page: *Our piece of tent fabric made a great difference to moving the sled when the direction of the wind was in our favour.*

John had constructed a wall from blocks of snow dug out of the wind pack to deflect the worst of the wind away from the tent. The 'snow wall' provided good protection against the wind—of that there was no doubt—but, in its lee, snow had accumulated two-thirds of the way up the back of the tent. Tiredness and impatience saw me kicking at the snow blocks weighing down the tent's valences with my hobnailed boots to break them loose. The first couple of blocks broke away obediently, but my boot went straight through the third, ripping a 10-centimetre hole in the fragile tent fabric as if it were wet paper. The tent pegs were buried deeply in drift behind the wall too, making them difficult to retrieve. The position of the pegs coupled with the fragility of the tent forced a more cautious approach to things.

To make matters worse, the pegs had actually frozen into the ice and stubbornly refused to move. A few gentle kicks to the first one sheared it completely, leaving just a frozen stump in the ice. I swore loudly. Today I just wanted things to be a bit easier but I knew they were not going to be. And so, as with so many things in the Antarctic, freeing the tent from its icy shackles became a major exercise. We worked on it like archaeologists on a dig, carefully chipping at the snow blocks with the blunt adze end of the ice axe, shaking and brushing away ice with gloved hands, and digging holes around each of the pegs with the spade. An exasperating hour later, with gloves soaked from contact with melted snow, the tent was finally rolled up and on the sled, still heavy with the weight of ice we had been unable to remove. We tied everything on and leaned into the harnesses for the first time in almost forty-eight hours.

It took a lot to budge the sled. The normal technique of my leaning heavily into the harness and John taking a 'run up' to jerk the sled into motion needed three attempts before the sled reluctantly started moving, the runners having frozen into place. I was exhausted, putting it down to having been immobile for two full days and the fact that we almost immediately had to climb through awkward sastrugi. The first couple of hours seemed to take forever. Lots of stop–start efforts of twenty minutes' duration with overheating and laboured breathing featured heavily. Finally we reached the top of a rise, justifying our hard work. Now the horizon stretched away further than we had yet seen to the south, our height—coupled with the clarity of the Antarctic air—giving us an uninterrupted view over the endless sea of white, hard snow pack, almost luminescent with the diffuse rays of the sun shining on it. The Pole lay almost 2500 kilometres distant with the coast a further 1500 kilometres beyond that. To our immediate west were the bristling turquoise crevasses of the Sorsdal glacier, menacing and deep and much like those that had swallowed Ninnis. Our route luckily took us inland, avoiding them, before turning west and travelling parallel to the coast.

Previous spread: *John's snow wall: surprisingly robust, as the blocks froze together once cut;*
opposite: *Another snow wall, far enough from the tent to prevent snow accumulating behind it and burying the tent.*

As we changed course from our mainly southerly route to the west, the wind now came over our left shoulders, as it had for Mawson as he headed west on his survival bid. John immediately suggested trying to harness the wind using our 'sail'— a small piece of old fabric that to date we had used to secure loose items of gear onto the sled, by using it as a cover and tying it down. Like Mawson, who fashioned a sail out of old clothes stitched together and used it to good effect, we cut holes in the corners of our sail and attached short guy ropes made from offcuts to them. I was sceptical about it making things much easier but persevered with slow fingers, cold and thick from inaction and exposure to the conditions. We secured a series of slideable prussic knots around the thicker guy lines that held the mast in position. This allowed crude adjustments to be made to the sail that we hoped would allow us to catch the polar wind more effectively, saving valuable time and energy while also reducing exposure of the hands. As we leaned into our harnesses again, it was a eureka moment, with any doubts I had had dispelled immediately. I had never used a sail before, having man-hauled for every step of every polar trip I had ever taken. Now it seemed as if a third person had suddenly started pulling alongside us. It felt unnatural but liberating as the wind that was so often our enemy was now put to good use. 'Like Ginger pulling still', said John jokingly, referring to Mawson's last dog.

I became convinced that using a sail, as do polar journeys in the modern era, must give teams a massive physical and psychological advantage. You could endure multiple bad days' man-hauling in the knowledge that when the wind was right you could cover some big ground using a modern sail. Even the small, old piece of fabric rigged crudely on the sled that we had made a big difference and we were grateful for the help.

By midnight we had covered a wonderful 18 kilometres, which lifted our mood hugely. It was still less than half of Mawson's best distance but neither that nor the cold in the tent could subdue our mood. That night I lay in my bag listening to the wind not as an adversary now but as a potential friend. 'Ginger' was out there and I went to sleep hoping she would remain with us for a while at least.

The next day the wind roared again from the south-east, heralding good things from our sail and in our minds more than compensating for the bitter cold we knew it would mean for us.

Opposite: *Adjusting the sail as quickly as possible with gloveless hands.*

John's prussic knots again allowed us to trim the sail by moving them up and down the guy lines. We assumed our normal positions and started to pull, but with both of us doing so from the front, the sled stubbornly slewed out to the side with the power of the wind in the sail. A boat has a keel to prevent this sideways yaw but the sled obviously didn't, meaning we had to fight almost as hard to keep the sled on course as we usually did to pull it normally. The wind was ferocious, meaning we had to don our hoods to keep sensation in our ears, making it almost impossible to hear one another. Added to the way the hoods narrowed our field of vision and caused our goggles to fog, it was frustrating work. Hand gestures and screamed instructions were needed before we reconfigured our positions. I continued out front with John at the rear pulling perpendicular to the way the sled was trying to go in order to keep it on track, stumbling as strong gusts of wind pulled him over. We trimmed and trimmed the sail until finally it was down altogether, the wind pushing the sled along on its own with our effort focused solely on keeping it on track. By day's end we had covered another 16

Opposite: *Mawson in a casual pose, with a fully laden sled that would have been pulled by a large dog team;*
above left: *Eating my Spartan ration during a break, back to the wind;*
above right: *A magical solar pillar—quite heavenly in appearance.*

kilometres and should have been happy, but we were exhausted, and the atmosphere in the tent was strangely subdued. We lay in our bags some hours later, feeling awed by Antarctica's power and its capacity to toy with our efforts. Today the wind had been with us. If we faced wind of this strength blowing against us, we would have no chance.

The tent was never going to go up in the wind as it was, so on arrival we moored the sled using the ice axes and quickly got to work digging out snow blocks to build another large wall. Both of us knew what was needed and worked silently, taking it in turns to dig out the blocks. I was sure I had lost a lot of weight and strength, although how much remained to be seen. I put it out of my mind and kept digging. The key was to get out of the wind. Quickly the wall took shape, deflecting away the worst of the wind and providing a haven in which to put up the tent. Finally, and with much protest, the tent was up. We secured two of the guy lines to the ice axes and fell grateful and exhausted into the tent's calm interior.

I recalled Mawson's trials and tribulations with the wind, both with Mertz and on his own. I re-read his diary, making note of the fact that he had winds from the south-east through to the east every single day after Ninnis' death and for more than a month until he experienced wind from the south-west and elsewhere with occasional storms. Frequently he just recorded the wind speed and direction, simple geography revealing that most of the time he had tail or cross winds. On other occasions he recorded how the 'wind helps' and 'had larger sail than usual', referring to how long he and Mertz were able to harness the tail wind. He also recorded that the wind made it 'very cold and laborious for Mertz rigging sail'. When Mawson was on his own, however, he wrote more than once that 'I dare not take down tent as could not get up again by myself'. Both with Mertz and on his own, Mawson's journey was to the west, with the wind either from the side—a 'broad reach'—or from directly behind him, allowing him to 'run with the wind'. Both were tail winds and of great assistance to him when he could use them.

Paradoxically, the wind had worked against him too. When the two men were together it made the conditions far colder, particularly for Mertz who had no windproof trousers. Often it also made visibility worse, difficult when trying to negotiate the potentially crevassed ground they sometimes faced.

Opposite: *The aftermath of a blizzard—snow and ice on one of the few guy lines;*
next page: *No shelter from the head wind as we lean into our work.*

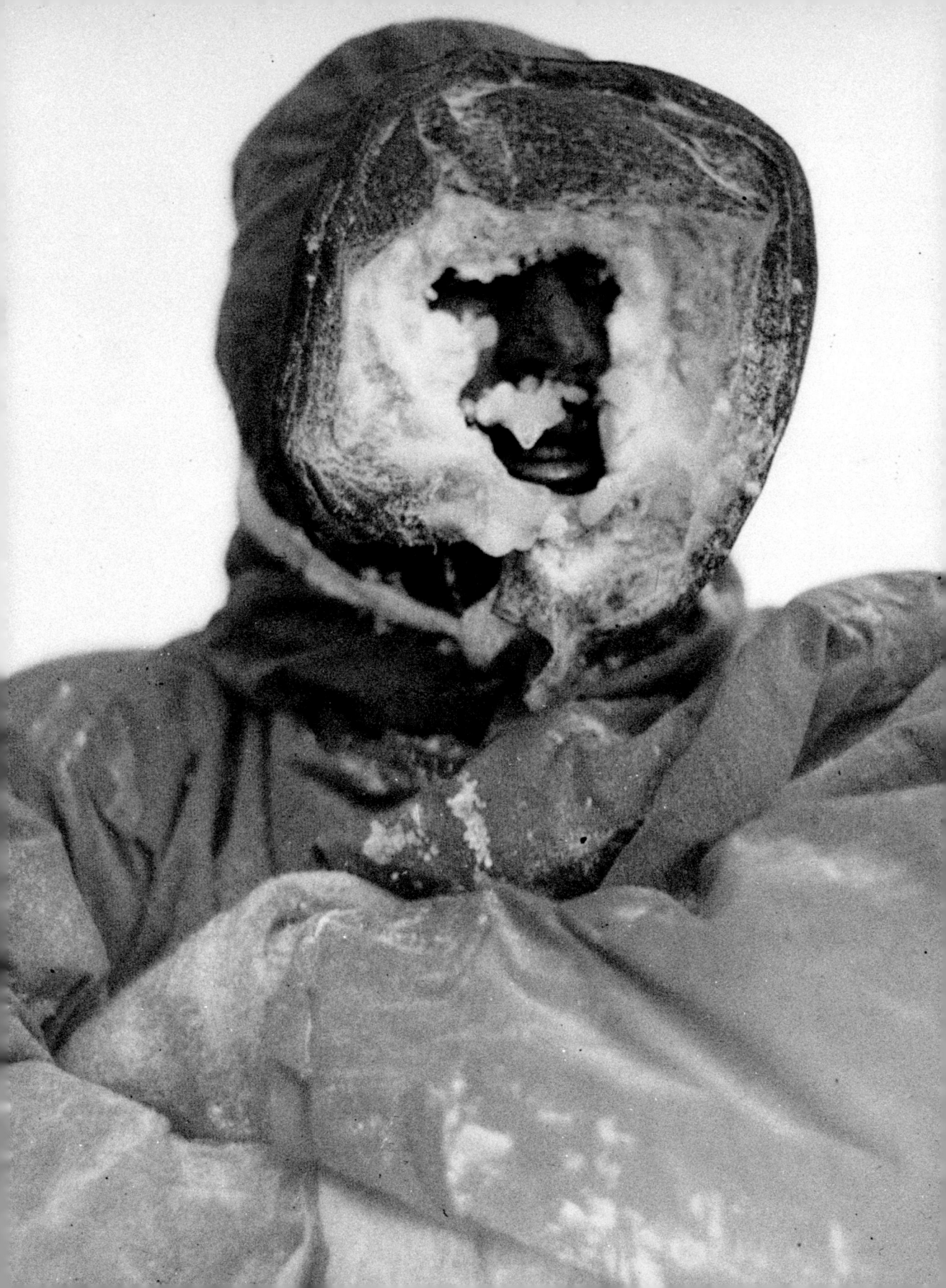

We woke to find that drift had come in through a large hole in the tent that had appeared overnight. The wind was too strong to fix the hole, so we pushed the tent box in front of it to staunch the draught and the steady inflow of snow. Even so, a bank of white completely covered the stove and John's feet. Even his normally calm countenance was ruffled, shocked at just how quickly Antarctica could reclaim even this little sanctum away from the elements. With hands numbed by the cold, John cleared away the snow, the conditions being too cramped for me to assist from my side. It added another hour to our day, with the stove needing a couple of extra infusions of meths to warm it enough to ignite the kerosene.

By early afternoon the wind had abated, allowing us the opportunity to work on our 'sailing technique'. The assistance the sail provided was welcome but the brain space it offered ironically allowed us more time to worry about things. Of particular concern was my plummeting weight—I could feel my clothes getting looser and my strength and cold tolerance beginning to wane. I think I had underestimated too the amount of butter we could have each day, it being difficult to accurately carve equal amounts daily from the tin with our original 1912 'Bonsa' knife. I suppose that was good news of a sort, knowing we could have a sliver more butter each day over the coming weeks. More worrying was that without the assistance of the sail on days where the wind was uncooperative, I was beginning to tire after three and a half hours, having to dig deep to get to four or four and a half hours. I had not defecated since Day 2 either, almost a week earlier, which was an indication that my body probably had nothing to spare. John, being smaller, fared only slightly better.

By Day 9, the wind and cold were rapidly approaching the most extreme conditions we had travelled in so far. The power of the wind against the side of the sled pulled us off balance even without the sail up. By four in the afternoon, it was only −10°C but desperately cold with a ferocious gale of 80 to 100 kilometres an hour. There was nowhere to shelter from it, and the only way to generate body heat was to keep moving, which required great effort. Something had to give. Moving to keep warm was all well and good, but the other part of that equation, the energy needed to fuel this, was lacking.

Previous page: *Ice accumulation around Burberry hoods, 100 years apart;*
opposite, left: *John drinking his fill before moving off again;*
opposite, right: *John, sheltering from the wind during a break. The sled provided the only barrier from the wind.*

The wind had again become our adversary. The Burberrys' tight cotton weave took the edge off it, although some got through, with John being particularly badly affected in only woollen trousers, and getting progressively colder despite our work. Gusts of wind toppled over the sled time and again like a toy, finally splintering the wooden bracket holding the mileage wheel. The loss of our sled wheel within a day of Mawson losing his, amongst the sastrugi on Day 8, convinced me that we were having similar experiences on our journey. I willed the similarities to end there, or things did not bode well for John or me for the five weeks we still had to endure.

5 Losing a Friend

The dreaded first medical came at the end of our tenth day on the ice. I felt depressed, with weight loss sitting heavily on my mind because it meant a reduction in our strength and ability to keep warm. It was also a real concern to me, as I had signed a pre-trip ethics agreement that a loss of 25 kilograms or more—the agreed limit of my decline in this coldest of places—meant the doctor would pull me out on medical grounds. . . .

The film crew would be on hand to film our first medical—a major intrusion into our lives. Not out of spite or malice, John and I had long since begun to regard interaction with them as something to be endured rather than welcomed, especially now, since we stood to find out how much we had declined, which would inevitably have effects on our morale. Proximity to the crew and their modern equipment only served to highlight just how different our situation was and distracted us from the task at hand. This, coupled with the fact that the crew failed to grasp the extent of the hardship and deprivation we were going through, made us feel somewhat resistant towards them.

Previous page: *The lonely plateau gives little back, forcing you to find the resolve from within.*

We trudged over to the polar pyramid tent set up for our medical. It was cold inside but quiet and still compared with our tent and its loosely flapping fabric. An hour of samples and measurements later, it was revealed that I had lost 6 kilograms and had some minor cold damage to my hands. I had expected the weight loss but it still left me worried as to whether I would continue to go down at this rate or whether it would accelerate. Either way I was on course for a loss of 25 kilograms by the forty-day mark and I would be forced to pull out before finishing the journey. I resolved to just do what I could. If that were enough, I would make it; if not, there would be nothing for me to be ashamed of. It was an unconvincing consolation, but the best I could muster.

John and I were soon back in our own—and Mawson's—world. On Day 12, undulating conditions and 'warm' weather flattered our pulling performance, but the following day brought bad luck, true to form. A significant amount of kerosene had leaked into the tent fabric while it was on the sled, courtesy of a poor seal on the fuel container—kerosene we could

Above left: *A lull in filming allows time to exchange thoughts;*
above centre: *The crew, dressed in all the colours of the rainbow, patiently wait for us to appear;*
above right: *Gale-force winds picking up.*

ill afford to lose and that subsequently could send the whole tent up in flames if we weren't careful. The bindings of the skis that formed half of our tent frame had ripped a 5-centimetre hole through the fabric during the night too, despite our having swathed them in fabric offcuts to safeguard against this happening. To add to our difficulties, fresh overnight snow made the sled runners stick, while white-out conditions meant a frustrating day stumbling around tripping over sastrugi, trying to focus on the compass and having the sled drag terribly. At least we knew where we were going; Mawson had not been so fortunate. He had undertaken his journey near the South Magnetic Pole, meaning the needle of his compass was dragged downwards to the source of magnetism directly beneath him, rendering it useless and forcing him to rely on the sun to navigate.

The next few days passed without great incident, although toil was our constant companion. John stitched up holes in the tent at roughly the same rate as new ones appeared, while we continued to nurse damp sleeping bags and rid ourselves of all non-essential items to save weight. For all its half-kilogram of weight, I never regarded Mawson's diary as non-essential: for me, it was critical to know what was going through his mind with all that was happening to him. What stood out more than anything was what was absent. His focus on the practical and logistical aspects of his experiences at the expense of more personal insights, while calamity and uncertainty reigned, spoke volumes about the discipline of the man.

For Mawson and Mertz, the two-week mark was a major turning point in their journey. Day 14 was the day that the final dog, Ginger, died. That night Mawson and Mertz dined on a supper of her brain and thyroids, using her skull as a bowl. They had both experienced significant weight loss, although exactly how much wasn't clear, but Mawson recorded for the first time doubts about his colleague's condition—'Xavier off colour'—on what was to become a rapid downward spiral for the normally robust Swiss.

John was also far from the top of his game. Despite his more modest weight loss, only 2 kilograms, he had been getting progressively worse as the days went by, his decline characterised by fatigue, what I perceived as moodiness, and a greatly reduced resistance to cold. Being from Siberia, he prided himself on his toughness in this respect, and I had seen plenty of evidence of it early in the trip. Now, though, on the many bitterly cold, windy days we endured, he wore not only his beaver-pelt gloves but also his woollen inner gloves and thick wool mitts beneath them, and was still cold. For a while he had been wearing these multiple layers not to keep warm but just to maintain some limited sensation in his hands in the desperate conditions, which were exacerbated by his not wearing any overtrousers. His pride in his Russian tolerance to cold had long since given way to the reality of his situation.

John was wearing the same clothes as Mertz had, eating the same amount of food and pulling a sled of the same weight in virtually identical conditions. In terms of differences, we perhaps had the advantage of slightly colder conditions and less fresh snowfall than they experienced, meaning we got less wet. But we had to pull without the assistance of dogs, as well as lug our dog-meat substitute along in the sled behind us—a negative evidenced by the modest distances we had managed. Yet Mertz was in far worse shape at this stage of the trip. The loss of his overtrousers certainly played a part, condemning him to perpetual wetness when the body heat he generated turned falling snow into water on contact, which then refroze as ice. Tent life too had been miserable for Mertz, with moisture from the dripping canvas of the tent and the melted snow beneath making him and Mawson progressively wetter despite their efforts.

Opposite: *Sastrugi. Each was 50 to 60 centimetres deep from peak to trough, and hard to pull a sled through.*

A Dog's Life

Sled dogs were an integral part of the exploration of Antarctica. In 1911 they hauled the supplies for Norwegian explorer Roald Amundsen, who was the first man to reach the South Pole, and of course they played a central part in Mawson's incredible journey of survival. Dogs are now banned from Antarctica by the 1993 Antarctic Treaty due to evidence that the canine disease distemper might be spreading to Antarctica's seals.

Sled dogs have remarkable strength for their size, being able to pull more than twice their weight for extended periods, with the best dogs tending to be 30 kilograms or smaller; larger dogs are at a physiological disadvantage for endurance travel. There are a number of different breeds, but the main ones used for sled pulling in Antarctica were the lighter weight Siberian husky, the heavier Alaskan malamute and cross-breeds of the two.

Mawson, Ninnis and Mertz had twelve dogs in two teams of six for their journey. With the loss of Ninnis and his dog team, this number was reduced to six dogs that were progressively killed and fed to the other dogs and the men. There was nothing unusual about this practice, in that weak or dying dogs were often fed to the other dogs even up to modern times. It was, however, unusual for polar explorers to eat dog flesh. Certainly native peoples in the Arctic would not eat the offal of animals, including dogs, knowing the consumption of their livers had adverse health effects.

Scott's failure to use sled dogs effectively is one of the most famous examples of how invaluable dogs were. Scott planned to reach the Pole using ponies, motorised sledges, and dogs in support, then by man-hauling. The motorised sledges failed; the ponies faltered, were put down and consumed; and the dogs were sent back to base camp halfway with most of the men. Scott and his four remaining colleagues then man-hauled to the Pole. These tactical errors (which Scott could not have foreseen) cost him and all of his South Pole team their lives. Amundsen, using dogs efficiently, beat Scott to the South Pole and survived to tell the tale.

Amundsen's expedition used dog teams to haul sledges while the five men in the party skied alongside. They used forty-two dogs to haul one-and-a-half tonnes of supplies, covering incredible distances, including climbing up onto the polar plateau: a 3000-metre climb in four days. The day that they arrived on the plateau, Amundsen ordered twenty-four of the dogs to be killed to provide food

for the remaining dogs and the men, something planned from the expedition's outset. Amundsen recorded his feelings as each man shot his dogs: 'A faithful servant lost his life for each shot . . . There was something oppressive, miserable in the air: We had grown so fond of our dogs'. He called this camp 'the Butcher's Shop'.

John and I found that we could not keep up with the distances Mawson and Mertz covered with their diminishing team of dogs over the course of the first two weeks of their survival bid. This is not surprising, in that a team of sled dogs can average around 10 kilometres an hour pulling a heavy load even in poor terrain. This is evidenced by the distances Mawson and Mertz covered in their first two weeks of travel despite the level of malnourishment of their dogs. Ginger and her companions may have poisoned Mawson and Mertz, but Mawson would not have made it without them.

Above: *Sledging stores up the ice slopes south of Cape Denison, with Ninnis in the lead.*

Mawson and Mertz were also younger than we were, far better acclimatised, and Mertz had moved along on skis for the first few days, unlike John, who had foot-slogged since the start. Mertz's rapid decline was a puzzle. Our thinking kept leading to the one really significant difference between the two men's experiences: the exact constitution of what they had eaten and, specifically, the fact that Mertz had eaten dog livers whereas John and I had not. Dog livers contain levels of vitamin A that are toxic to humans if consumed in sufficient quantity, and the conventional hypothesis is that Mertz may have poisoned himself in this manner. It was still too early to say, but it was beginning to look as though the theory held some water.

I had never really been a fan of 'silver bullet' theories that conveniently explain away everything, as the vitaminosis theory did in the case of Mawson and Mertz, finding it too simple a solution. I felt that, of the six dogs that Mawson and Mertz had had with them, several would have been fed to the other dogs, leaving perhaps a liver each for the men, and that it was unlikely that Mertz would die from the vitamin A contained within his share. Now, although John was suffering from fatigue, moodiness and reduced resistance to cold, he was spared Mertz's worst symptoms—hallucinations, fever and total exhaustion—forcing me to reconsider.

For some reason, my cold tolerance remained reasonable, something I put down to the fact that, being bigger, I had a larger volume-to-surface ratio than John. My principal problem was loss of strength and general fatigue through my more rapid weight loss. Now towards the end of each day, even routine, incidental tasks like digging snow blocks for the tent valances were difficult for me, and it was always me and not John who tired first.

Like two half-men we trudged along, working as one to keep our momentum going. The Burberrys did the best they could to shield us from the wind and we routinely wore the hoods over our balaclavas to reduce the wind chill that threatened our ears with frostbite. Our goggles misted over with the moisture from our heavy breathing and it quickly froze, obscuring our vision, meaning that we had to tilt our heads at strange angles in order to find clear sections of glass to see through. Nothing was easy.

Opposite: *Tying everything down as securely as possible as a blizzard approaches.*

Our priorities had changed now and we catered for one another's requirements as best we could. I needed more frequent breaks to consume at least some food to keep me going. John, on the other hand, couldn't afford to stop for too long for fear of getting even colder hands. We therefore conducted breaks quickly, with the two of us slumped on the snow in the lee of the sled to get away from the biting wind that sought us out. As we stared blankly downwind, our backs against the sled, snow roared past at either end, hugging the contours of the ground as it rushed towards a distant horizon. I would cram a handful of raisins and a boiled sweet into my mouth to try to keep my energy levels up, while John kept his gloved hands as warm as possible under his armpits. Scarcely moments after we had sat down, Antarctica, devoid of any compassion for our predicament, prodded us mercilessly to lift our tired bodies to move on again.

John sometimes walked leeward of me so that I shielded him from the winds of more than 50 kilometres an hour that we faced, helping him to keep warmer and preserve his hands. At the end of a day's effort, he would, with his remaining energy, help me to dig snow blocks in addition to his own job of erecting the tent. Teamwork was excellent but progress excruciating, in the form of small, painfully won steps to cover the 14 or so kilometres a day we had to travel. All the time I fought the notion that working so hard on so little food was simply prolonging the inevitable: the day when we would not be able to keep going for lack of energy.

As John and I lay deep within our sleeping bags after Day 15, we discussed our ongoing problems with sled drag. It was puzzling why the runners hadn't been varnished, which would have helped them to glide more easily. To add to the problem, the sastrugi had cut up the runners, making them even less disposed to moving easily. By the time tiredness ended our conversation, John and I had decided to sacrifice light and warmth, and use our candles to wax the runners. Luckily, the weather on the next day proved good enough for us to put our plan into action. We removed the snow block from the lee side of the tent and dragged half of the sled into our cramped quarters. We heated our bowl over the stove and dripped the wax onto the bases, working it as best we could with the underside of the bowl.

Opposite: *Waxing the runners of the sled, one half at a time, in a desperate bid to reduce drag.*

Over the course of an hour and a half, we lubricated the runners. Mertz had carried out a similar job, using tar, on the runners of their sled.

Our reward was a slight improvement in drag. Of course, perhaps it was all psychological and we were simply willing it to be better. Improvement or not, the key thing was that we were at least doing all we could to improve our situation and that kept us positive.

By the end of Day 16 we had covered a total of just under 200 kilometres; some 100 kilometres behind where Mawson and Mertz had been at the same time. We had had poor visibility for the past few days: white-out or near white-out conditions. We used the orientation of the sastrugi to navigate, the faint shadow they cast acting as a pointer. Antarctica is predictable at least in terms of wind direction, such that even in poor light, if you can discern a slight shadow behind a ridge of sastrugi you can often work out what direction you are heading.

But we were slowly gaining on Mawson and Mertz. Our gains were not, however, down to our travelling fast but due to the fact that Mawson and Mertz by this stage were travelling incredibly slowly. Their distances after the death of Ginger on Day 14 had plummeted, though the cause of this was unclear: whether it was the loss of Ginger, Mawson and Mertz's consumption of the dog livers, the effect of the wet and cold on Mertz, or some combination of these factors.

We were due for our second medical. This time John had lost more weight but was taking it philosophically. My condition was not so good. I had lost 10 kilograms more in only a week—more than a kilogram a day—an extremely rapid loss by anyone's standards. Suddenly I was only 8 kilograms away from elimination on medical grounds and I worried now that the decision of whether or not to stop would not be mine to make. In order to slow my weight decline, I decided to steal a little from the future rations to give me extra each day: no different from what Mawson had done, eating varying quantities depending on his day's effort. Without more food, there would be no future. I took the equivalent of about a day's worth spread over two weeks, a trifling amount by normal standards. My extra rations comprised a piece of sledge biscuit and a quarter teaspoon of sugar a day. The amounts were pitifully small but I still didn't like doing it, feeling uneasy consuming even a small amount of food above my carefully calculated daily schedule. My food intake was one of the only constants in a world where I controlled very little else.

No blizzards, my slightly increased food intake and John's desire to finish strongly meant that we closed again on Mawson and Mertz. By the end of Day 22 we were within 28 kilometres of their total of 320 kilometres. Mertz by this stage was desperately unwell, having declined spectacularly from being, in Mawson's words, 'off-colour' and 'not his usual cheerful self' on Day 16 to being routinely unable to get out of his sleeping bag to do anything. Mawson recorded on Day 22: 'A long and wearisome night. If only I could get on. But I must stop with Xavier, and he does not appear to be improving—both our chances are going now'.

Shortly after eating the dog-meat, Mertz would complain to Mawson about it, saying that 'he had found [it] very disagreeable and felt that he was getting little nutriment [sic] from it'. Mertz suggested that 'we should abstain for a time from eating any further of this meat'. Whether he just intensely disliked it or had some vague realisation that it could be doing him real harm is unclear. Mawson also records that he was experiencing a dull, gnawing pain in the abdomen and that changing position as he rested seemed to improve it. He attributed the pain to their stomachs being empty and acids attacking the stomach lining. Mawson was of the opinion that movement served in some way to redistribute the concentration of the acids, alleviating the pain. Whether Mawson too was suffering toxicity caused by eating the dog livers is unclear.

In the meantime, the effects I was experiencing included rapid weight loss, constant hunger, susceptibility to the cold and being seemingly stuck in second gear when it came to pulling the sled. Despite all this, I had not had the chronic stomach pain and skin and hair loss that Mawson had experienced. My journey had obviously diverged considerably from Mawson's, as John's had from Mertz's. The common denominator again appeared to be the dog livers.

Other problems had surfaced, however. A large hole had developed in my right boot, caused by my scuffing one hobnailed boot against the other in poor visibility. It was enough to make me lose all sensation in my right big toe. Despite keeping my toe as warm as possible in the sleeping bag at night, sensation had refused to return to it to the extent that I had no idea what state it was in. For the previous two days, I had therefore worn a normal leather boot on my left foot and the warmer reindeer-skin boot, or finnesko, on the right to try to keep that foot warmer, and to slow the decline. Although it kept my foot warm, the finnesko lacked grip and caused me to fall several times. With the tunnel vision brought on by our hoods and iced-up goggles, the only indication John often had that I had fallen and was no longer

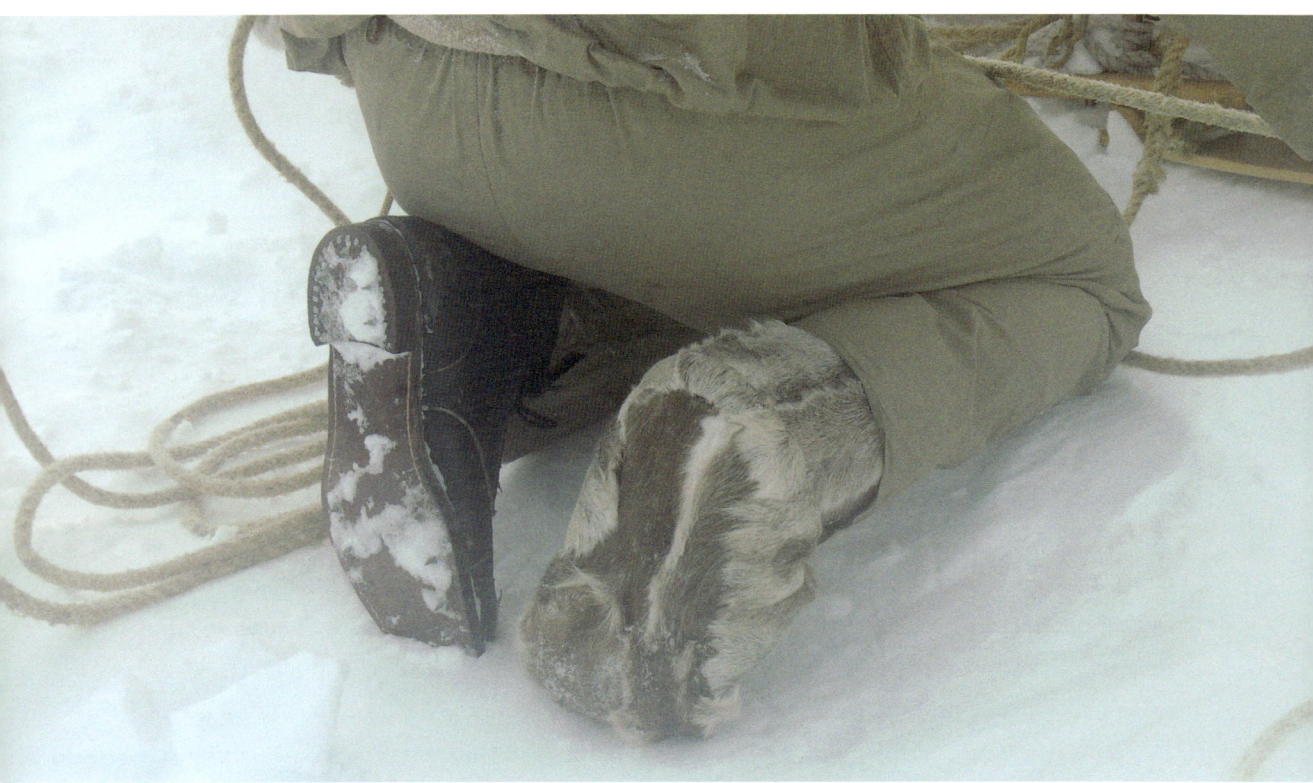

pulling was sudden inertia from the sled. We now had 17.5 kilometres to go until we reached the magic 320-kilometre mark—the distance Mawson and Mertz had covered at the point that Mertz died.

We arrived a day earlier than Mawson and Mertz had, as they had had a day of inaction due to Mertz's deterioration. In accordance with our expedition's methodology, John was to leave at the point that Mertz died: after either twenty-five days or 320 kilometres—whichever came first—and I was to continue on for the remaining twenty-one days or just over 160 kilometres alone, as Mawson had done.

I had been putting off thinking too much about what it would be like, psychologically, to travel without John, restricting my thoughts to the practicalities of life on my own: making camp, pulling the sled and so on, and not about the effects of loneliness or solving problems with one head instead of two. Antarctica, much like the sea, is amongst the loneliest of places, and this would test me to the limit.

By this point, things were looking dire for Mawson. He wrote:

> *Things are in a most serious state for both of us—if he [Mertz] cannot go on 8 or 10 m [13.5 to 16 km] a day, in a day or two we are doomed. I could pull through myself with the provisions at hand but I cannot leave him. His heart seems to have gone. It is very hard for me—to be within 100 m [160 km] of the Hut and in such a position is awful.*

Mawson dressed Mertz ready to make the most of reasonable weather facing them but Mertz was in no fit state to move, having, in Mawson's words 'a kind of a fit'. Mawson continued: 'This is terrible. I don't mind for myself but it is for Paquita [Mawson's fiancée] and for all the others connected with the expedition that I feel so deeply and sinfully. I pray to God to help us.'

This is the first and only time that Mawson spoke of God, although two days earlier, on Day 23, in reference to their poor chances of survival, he wrote: 'All will depend on Providence now—it is an even race to the hut'.

I find Mawson's single mention of God and subsequent references to Providence revealing. It was effectively his way of admitting that, as tough and resourceful as he was, much of the responsibility for his survival relied on forces greater than him 'allowing' him to succeed. Thus far on his journey, it had been his ingenuity, determination and dedication to routine and order that had got him as far as he had—all good, solid Edwardian values. But now it was down to 'Providence': luck, destiny, the personification of Antarctica as some omnipotent, sentient thing, or, even bigger than that—God. Whatever the case, Mawson now saw his survival as depending on the judgement of some bigger, compassionate force. For me, Mawson had gone from being a man who believed in God but relied on himself to being a man who was increasingly accepting that his day-to-day fate was firmly in the hands of his maker.

Opposite: *Wearing my finnesko on my right foot to try to halt frostbite.*

I am not entirely certain about my feelings on the subject. I believe in something bigger than myself and, if pushed on the matter, am comfortable with this authority being called 'God'. I have certainly felt at several points during my life when alone and faced with a seemingly insurmountable problem that I have been helped by someone or something, and it has certainly happened out on the ice. My more sceptical side explains this as being a more resourceful part of myself that comes to the fore when faced with such adversity—a part of me that is sufficiently unfamiliar for me to think it is another. My instincts, however, tell me it is something else. Perhaps Providence or God is closer to the mark.

A small camp, no more than a dot on the horizon, marked the position of the film crew that awaited our arrival at the 320-kilometre mark. We approached with trepidation, with little chance now to really talk about what we had been through before the cameras were upon us. John voiced what I was thinking: we had been through incredible turmoil as we had tried to grapple with the problems, insecurities and worry of imminent equipment or personal failure on the expedition—especially when compounded by a starvation diet and 100-year-old technology. The ability to cope with all of this was the result of the strength of the relationship between us: a strong bond based on trust and a solid friendship.

It was to our minds remarkable how warmth, plentiful food, modern equipment and motorised travel utterly removed others from the experience we were having. I likened it to bystanders watching marathon runners going through a private hell, grappling with mental and physical pain as they fight to keep their tired bodies moving. Observers can witness the grimaces on the runners' faces and the heaviness of their step and hear their laboured breathing, yet still be a world away from understanding the battle going on inside the runners' heads and how heavy the prospect of personal failure weighs.

Central to the success of any expedition such as this is the ability to keep negative thoughts under control and to focus on positives. Practically, this meant not even uttering concerns, as doing so made them seem more real and less easy to put behind us, a problem exarcerbated by the film crew's desire to discuss our problems with us in great detail.

Opposite: *The Rusky's journey is over—a job well done;*
next page: *Alone now with only my own thoughts and determination to keep me going.*

Our final steps to the waiting film crew were taken with mixed emotions. John's relief and laughter at having finished were real as he received their congratulations, while I stood quietly in the background, deep in thought and faced with the magnitude of how the new logistics of solo travel would work. I was genuinely happy for John. He had upheld his end of the bargain, battling the elements without the extra protection of overtrousers that I had had, and had done much of the repair work to our tent and stove in order to keep them functioning. He had done so uncomplainingly, a stoic and tough companion whose humour had helped to sustain us through some dark moments on the expedition. He was a proud man, and deserved to be for his performance on the journey. Now he would be with me no more and I would miss him as a good friend and trusted companion. Mawson's words now echoed in my head, summing up my predicament: 'All will depend on Providence now—it is an even race to the hut'.

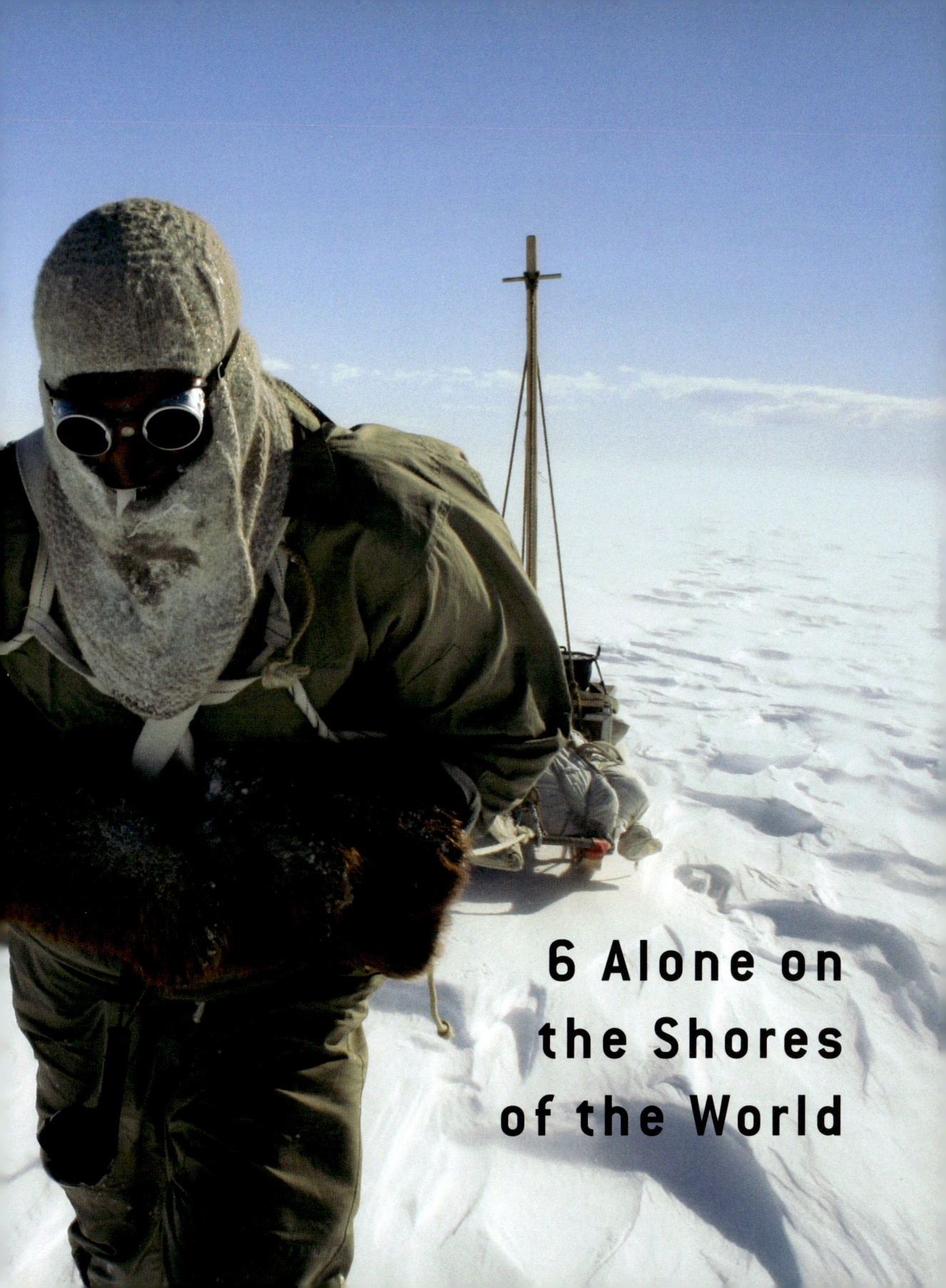

6 Alone on the Shores of the World

Mawson records the ordeal of Mertz's final hours:

. . .

During the afternoon he has several fits & is delirious, fills his trousers again and I clean out for him. He is very weak, becomes more and more delirious, rarely being able to speak coherently. Continues to rave and call for hours. I hold him down, then he becomes more peaceful & I put him quietly in the bag. He dies peacefully at about 2 a.m. on morning of 8th. Death due to exposure finally bringing on a fever, result of weather exposure & want of food. He had lost all skin of legs & private parts. I am in same condition & sores on finger won't heal.

Previous page: *My balaclava, heavy with frozen moisture from breathing hard, was like chain mail around the face.*

Mawson did not dwell on the loss of Mertz—at least, he did not articulate any thoughts in his diary, instead shifting his concern to his chances of survival, which he regarded as slim:

> *I have left Xavier in his bag and taken him outside to bury ... For many days now Xavier's condition has prevented us going on and now I am afraid it has cooked my chances altogether, even of a single attempt either to the coast or to the Hut—lying in the damp bag for a week on extremely low rations has reduced my condition seriously. However, I shall spend today remodelling the gear to make an attempt. I shall do my utmost to the last for Paquita's & supporters & members of expedition's sakes, and at least get word through how matters stand. I hope to get off in good time with reasonable weather tomorrow ...*

Ironically the next day's weather meant no travel for Mawson, due mainly to the strength of the wind and his consequent fear of not being able to put the tent up again if he broke camp. This afforded him time at least to 'read the Burial service over Xavier'. The weather was much better the day after that, although curiously Mawson again decided to stay put to give his wounds a chance to heal. Given that most of his injuries were the result of wet conditions and lack of food, and that staying another day consigned him to more of the same, I wondered whether some of his reluctance to leave Mertz's side was due to feelings of guilt or remorse at being the sole survivor. Aside from Mawson's weak physical condition, and his fear of becoming separated from his tent, he was certainly in no hurry to leave.

Mawson would have buried Mertz right next to the tent, separated from the cadaver by only a thin piece of fabric as he lay there that night alone. I had always thought the natural reaction in Mawson's position would be to want to get away, so that there would be a glimmer of hope of making it back alive and to literally create distance from the terrible event. Perhaps, however, it would be perfectly natural, having lost someone so close to you, to want to remain with them a little longer, especially given that Mawson and Mertz had endured so much together. With the wind buffeting my tent as I lay there, I wondered if I would have paid my final respects and left as soon as possible or stayed a while. It was not difficult to imagine the body of a fallen colleague providing at least some source of companionship on the vast, lonely plateau.

Opposite: *Deep in thought.*

After John's departure, certainly my situation was paralleling Mawson's in terms of having an extended period of inaction in the tent. But a shout over the howl of the wind from beyond the wall of fabric alerted me to the fact that I wasn't truly alone. A not inconsequential amount of spindrift later and the cameraman was inside my now relatively roomy abode, his vibrant colours and camera lights incongruous amidst the drab 1912 surroundings. The camera rolled, zooming in on my drawn face as he calmly relayed the news that a ferocious blizzard would hit us in a matter of hours. It meant no chance of travel and a good chance of some minor calamity for me in my old tent. He patiently waited for an adverse reaction—at worst a look of concern or frustration, at best some kind of meltdown at the cruelty of the timing of this latest piece of bad luck. None came. I shrugged, muttering words about my being here to test myself in precisely these conditions, it having been after all precisely what Mawson had experienced. I believed my response, although I suspect my philosophical tone might not have been what he wanted to hear.

I had anticipated the blizzard. The steady increase in wind strength since the merciful lull of a few hours earlier that had allowed me to erect the tent was a telltale sign. Now, more than

Previous page: *Feeling the strain;*
above: *Guy lines are fixed and a snow wall built for the ensuing blizzard;*
next page: *Placing snow blocks on the tent valances with a weather front approaching.*

I had at the loss of John, I felt very alone. In the lead up to going solo I had reminded myself how important it would be to establish a new routine immediately after his loss, the routine of travel being the best way to give me some order in amongst the formlessness of it all. With the bad weather consigning me to the tent, that had not happened.

I was feeling extremely isolated and the occasional presence of the film crew offered surprisingly little solace. I expended a lot of mental energy in the tent just remaining calm and patient and reminding myself of what had been achieved already on the journey. I had started getting used to feeling lonely in the few days before John had left. He had understandably started to become focused on finishing as we crept up on Mawson and Mertz, and had begun to relax about the extent of deterioration in his gear, body and soul because of the short distance he had left to travel. Although it was a natural reaction on his part and I knew he would be with me in spirit on my solo journey, our expeditions had been on a divergent path for some time as I psychologically prepared myself for going solo.

Now I was high on the polar plateau alone, bar limited interaction with people who to me at the time seemed unconcerned as to whether I made it or not. Their goal was to get a good film product: that meant drama and not necessarily success. Partly due to starvation, I started to lose perspective, with paranoia setting in. I convinced myself that heroic failure would make for better drama—as would my gradual unravelling—as the reality of my predicament hit me.

My failure too would give credence to the fact that Mawson's journey could not be completed on the rations and dog-meat alone, and would give weight to the accusations of cannibalism made against Mawson at the time. In the years immediately after the expedition, many articles directly accused him of needing to have cannibalised Mertz in order to have had sufficient food to make the journey after Ninnis' death in the crevasse weeks earlier. 'Man eats dog and man', 'Could eat corpse but he buries it and lives 39 days on dog' and 'Unlucky companion's body tempted hungry explorer' were the headlines of newspapers in Australia and the USA at the time. The number of days Mawson remained by Mertz after his death did little to dispel the rumours.

Personally I did not believe he did it because he said as much at the time. It would of course have been in his interests to deny it, particularly given the sensibilities of the period.

Was Mawson a Cannibal?

After the death of Ninnis, Mawson and Mertz were left with only ten days of normal 'sledging rations' each and six dogs with no food: total rations of 395 grams made up of 170 grams of sledging food and supplemented by 225 grams of dog meat each. This they survived on for twenty-five days, until Mertz died. After his tragic death, Mawson's daily intake (for the next twenty-one days) rose fractionally to 450 grams, still less than half the normal ration, with much of the food of low energy value. This would have been extremely difficult to survive on even if he had been fit and the remaining journey had gone well. But he had to endure the most harrowing journey imaginable, including hurricane-force winds, blizzards and several near-misses with crevasses. Unsurprisingly, his health suffered as a result.

Rumours abounded at the time about Mawson having either eaten or been tempted to eat Mertz. Having trekked unsupported to the South Pole in forty-seven days myself, consuming 29 400 kilojoules a day, I lost more than 17 kilograms or about 20 per cent of my body weight. Even though my journey distance was longer, I wondered what it must have taken Mawson to survive on a journey of the same duration on less than a third of the kilojoules. I became interested to see if I could accomplish the journey without having to eat supplementary food—which would have been the equivalent of cannibalising Mertz's body.

The hypothesis behind my journey was not dissimilar to that of explorer Thor Heyerdahl who sailed a primitive balsa wood raft, the *Kon-Tiki*, from South America to Polynesia in 1950 to prove that Stone Age humans could have colonised Polynesia from South America. Like him, if I successfully completed the journey, I would prove it *could* have happened but (significantly) not that it definitely *did*.

I hoped too that by exposing myself to some of the

Even in the modern era, with our very changed attitudes to so many things, cannibalism is still beyond the pale for most. I agree with those who knew Mawson, such as the former head of the Australian Antarctic Division, Dr Philip Law, who felt he could have done it but that he did not. Caught between life and death in similar circumstances to Mawson, I believe I would entertain it; although, to know for sure, you would have to be faced with it as a desperate reality.

Whatever happened, Mawson's diet for the next three weeks was between half and a third of the normal sledging ration of 960 grams of 'concentrated rich food' the men had started with. This would have been extremely difficult to survive on even if Mawson had been fit and the remaining journey had gone smoothly. But he had to endure the most harrowing journey imaginable. Not only had he suffered the tremendous psychological blow of having lost both of his colleagues, but he also faced low temperatures, hurricane-force winds, blizzards and several near-fatal crevasse falls.

On polar expeditions, due to the harshness of the conditions, you play all sorts of mental tricks to keep yourself going, operating for much of the time in a very altered reality. Alone that night in the tent as the wind grew stronger, I convinced myself somewhat self-importantly that it was down to me to try to protect Mawson's honour by making it. No one was going to pin cannibalism on him, and certainly not based on my shortcomings. I knew then and there I had hit on something I could use to bolster my mental resolve and I felt Mawson would have approved.

All through the night and into the following morning the wind raged. The noise in the tent was intense as loose canvas flapped madly on its crude frame. Spindrift poured in through the multiple holes, the stove played up, and I again lay dressed in all my clothes, fearful that the tent might either tear open or blow away altogether during the night. Curiously, I was becoming familiar with this feeling and, although I worried, I neither turned to panic nor allowed it to affect my judgement. The fact that I had already survived one night of ferocious blizzard coupled with the fact that I didn't feel as lonely as I thought I would lifted my mood. This relative control bred a strange sense of calm, making me feel quite philosophical about

Opposite: *Organising my meagre belongings.*

my predicament. The 'even race' to the finish was not my journey against Mawson's as I had initially thought it would be, but he and I against the ticking clock and Antarctica. With the realisation about failure and its repercussions for him, I felt Mawson would be there in principle if not in spirit to support me too. I would sit this out and would not allow myself to become despondent.

My next major concern was that I had not taken a single step since John's departure and didn't know how the sled would load let alone move with just me pulling it. I had cut the sled in half almost three days previously, agonising over where to make my incision as if I were operating on a feeling, sentient being. Too far back and the friction of the sled runners would have made the sled too hard to pull. Too far forward and it would have been too unstable and small to carry my remaining items through the rough sastrugi. It still sat untested, somewhere in the blizzard only metres from the tent.

Previous page: *Pulling into the teeth of the wind;*
above left: *The crew filming;*
above right: *Moving away from camp in deteriorating conditions, keen to cover ground.*

It seemed, despite my generally philosophical mood, that I always still had room for a predetermined level of stress about something. If it wasn't an issue I had to face immediately, it was the prospect of one, with my mind seemingly having a certain capacity for worry regardless of the magnitude of the problems facing me.

I repaired things, ate my full ration and slept as the hours ticked by interminably. The wind strength grew at about the same rate as my mood again deflated. I tried to focus on the positives of the past two days since John had left in order to strengthen up mentally. I had successfully cut down the sled with my knife—a proud moment using the sword blade on an original Bonsa knife. I had reattached the ropes to the reduced sled so that I could still use the sail, and 'moored' the sled with a couple of clove hitch knots through some of the tent pegs so that it would not blow away during the night. My temperamental stove was going well after considerable protest, having become clogged with fuel residues and melted snow, and my snow wall, for now at least, seemed to be withstanding the onslaught. I repeated these positives like a mantra to lift my mood.

Mawson at this stage was pessimistic about his chances of survival much as I was now about being able to cover the remaining ground successfully. For him, his regrets seem to have stemmed from his choice of route: 'As there is little chance of my reaching human aid alive I greatly regret my inability to set out the coast line as surveyed for the 300 miles [483 kilometres] we travelled and record the notes on glaciers and ice formations'. Whether he meant this from the point of view of a scientific opportunity missed or for the logistics of his using the coastal route to return by is unclear. Either way he seems curiously detached about the prospect of not making it, much as his contemporary Scott had been only the year before, coolly describing his imminent death in a letter to his wife: 'I wasn't a very good husband, but I hope I shall be a good memory …'

Mawson's moods understandably ebbed and flowed between being circumspect about death and disarmingly frank about his slim chances of survival and allowing this to drag him into despondency. These were feelings that echoed my own sentiments, although the stakes were of course very different. Mawson wrote:

> *For hours I lay in the bag, rolling over in my mind all that lay behind and the chance of the future. I seemed to stand alone on the wide shores of the world … My physical condition was such that I felt I might collapse at any moment … Several of my toes commenced to blacken and fester near the tips and the nails worked loose. There appeared to be little hope … It was easy to sleep on in the bag, and the weather was cruel outside.*

The blizzard raged into its fourth day as I also lay in my tent deep in thought. I had at least two weeks to go and by now my journey closely paralleled Mawson's. I lay there: warm enough but damp, uncomfortable and on edge, thinking about what these delays would cost me in the final analysis and still wearing all my clothes as a precaution. Although I was not in as bad a physical state as Mawson had been, my feet were nevertheless starting to deteriorate seriously, with permanent numbness in several of the toes on my right foot, blackening of the skin on the bases of both feet, joint pain, and blisters on my heels from rubbing against frozen, unyielding leather.

Mid-way through my fourth day after John's departure, coincidentally just as Mawson had experienced, the wind began to abate and I decided to move. I was sick of the inaction,

gnawing hunger and worry. Sluggish, I lifted myself out of my bag, rolling it into a sodden, uncooperative weight in the corner of the tent. There were now so many things to think about. Once outside the tent, movement had to be fast and decisive to avoid getting too cold. That would be difficult given how damp I was, the force of the wind, and how much my metabolism seemed to have slowed following almost four days in the bag.

And the routine of loading the sled was new to me. There would be less weight, as it no longer carried John's possessions, and it was now only half as long as it had been, but the fixed weights of the tent, stove, boxes and fuel remained. Loading all these items onto a far smaller sled now constituted my next challenge.

Digging the tent and sled out of the snow and ice and loading all of my remaining possessions took almost an hour and a half. At least the dampness in my clothes froze within the first twenty minutes or so, making them impervious to the icy wind, if not like a suit of armour then one of chain mail at the very least—stiff and unmalleable, the fabric like cardboard chafing against the skin around the neck and wrists.

Above left: *Focusing hard to make sure I make no mistakes;*
above right: *Manoeuvring a tent pole into position.*

I leaned into the harness, unsure what to expect. Slowly the sled moved, complete with boxes roughly tied and the tent that now protruded about a metre out from its prow like a jouster's lance. To my pleasant surprise, the wind had shifted round to behind me and that, combined with the icy flat ground, made the sled move relatively easily. I felt an overwhelming sense of freedom. Within minutes this had become elation as I began to believe, for now, at least, that I could finally complete this journey. By day's end this had translated into the best distance of the trip, around 20 kilometres—a combination of a pent-up release of energy, a longer-than-usual sledging day, and favourable conditions, including a roaring tail wind.

My good mood, and my blistered feet, to some extent at least mirrored Mawson's state at this stage of his journey: 'the whole of both feet having formed large blisters and burst … feet in a deplorable condition … If Providence can give me 20 days weather like this and my feet can heal quickly surely I can reach succour'. On Day 23, when Mawson had first mentioned Providence, it seemed that it was in response to the realisation that Mertz's poor condition was condemning them both. As sad as Mertz's death had been, 'Providence' now appeared to be offering Mawson a chance to live. Although he never would have spoken of it as such, Mertz's death had given Mawson a kind of deliverance.

From all my polar travels, there is one key thing I try not to forget: never allow a journey to become a personal battle with the place. The reasons for this are twofold: you cannot afford to wage war with Antarctica, quite simply because you will never win. It will absorb all of your energy, resolve, inventiveness, anger, pain and exhilaration with ease. Second, it is both ridiculous and counter-productive to assign human values to such a place. Anthropocentrism or personification of events that happen to you as if they are in some way behavioural is pointless. If you do, it is easy to see the problems and danger as being designed to thwart your efforts. Completely at odds with this, on that day I had difficulty in not feeling Antarctica had been kind to me, providing me with mental breathing space—a chance to stand back and remember what I was doing here, what this place meant to me and to appreciate its stark beauty and the reasons for embarking on the challenge.

That night, happy with my day's effort and the pitch of the tent, and with a boiled sweet in my mouth, I made my most optimistic diary entry yet, belying the almost three full days of delays that were now miraculously being consigned to memory.

I can do this, and feel I have energy aplenty for whatever challenges may come tomorrow. I am in the company of that more resourceful side of my character. I know this good mood will pass but for now I feel mentally strong and very happy.

As much as I missed the camaraderie with John, my mood also came in part from the tremendous sense of purpose and satisfaction I got from moving under my own steam.

The daily routine now consisted of a hot cup of tea with all of my day's sugar in it to get myself going, followed by a weak hooch of kangaroo jerky and lard—unpalatable, but it filled the stomach with liquid at least. The food for the rest of the day consisted of a weak cocoa mix with a small knob of butter, a small handful of raisins and a few boiled sweets. This meagre amount needed to fuel four hours or so of sled-pulling towards an endless white horizon, through rough, windblown waves of sastrugi. If I were lucky, in the evening I would still have a handful of jerky left to eat raw, washed down with a weak tea made with the reused tea bag. Hunger, though, had inexplicably diminished a little from the week before—perhaps my stomach had shrunk and now needed far less to fill it, or perhaps because I was taking a small amount from future rations in the form of a few more raisins and a little more jerky. I just hoped it was enough to stabilise my weight and prevent my losing the kilogram a day that I had during the first few weeks.

Cruelly but predictably, the positive mood I had been cultivating did not last. I was woken from deep sleep by the sensation of something cold around my face. The tent was cold and dark. Through the steam of my breath I noticed that the tent door had come undone and was flapping wildly, affording me full view of the white tumult outside. Over my shoulder was a neat pile of snow, deposited there through a hole in the tent that had appeared behind my head. I sat up in the bag and grappled with the fabric of the door, tying it shut. The hole behind me could not be fixed, such was the tension in the tent: my attempts to do so with needle and twine served only to numb the fingers and make the hole tear further. A stopgap measure involved a rolled-up sock forced into the hole. I brushed the snow from my bag and lay awake as the wind howled malevolently. It was difficult not to take the environment personally. I wanted to be anywhere but here.

7 False Start

This second blizzard was even more devastating than the first, as the day's lull had raised my hopes. I had let my guard down, believing that, after such a ferocious storm, several days of calm might follow. How wrong I was. Like Mawson, who dared not take his tent down for fear of being unable to erect it again, I hoped now that the wind would not do the job of taking my tent down for me. Major doubts resurfaced in my mind about whether I could make it. A few more stormy days like this would mean that the answer was a resounding 'no'.

. . .

The all-too-familiar sensation of inaction in the tent was again upon me. Lying waiting for the slightest hints that the wind might be abating proved futile, with periods of momentary calm followed immediately by its increasing in strength. My diary told me that my third medical was due. While I welcomed it as a means of taking my mind off the inaction, I wasn't sure how bad news about my health would affect my fragile mood.

My mind drifted to thinking about how Mawson, despite the trauma of Mertz's death, made little mention of it for the rest of his journey. A large part of this must have been due to his

Previous page: *The frustration of being tent-bound again, with food fast running out.*

desire to put it all behind him and focus on the future, and to the fact that he was too beset with his own problems to dwell on past events. I wondered whether a significant part of it may also have related to feelings of guilt over a subconscious sense of relief that Mertz had not definitively condemned him to death.

This is partly reflected in Mawson's changes in mood about his chances. He had gone from fearing that his opportunity of reaching safety had vanished to an optimism—within days of Mertz's death—that, with favourable conditions, he could make it back.

As they had been to Mawson, big mood swings were very familiar to me. What differed significantly between us was the extent to which we had physically declined. Mawson wrote of himself: 'My whole body is apparently rotting from want of proper nourishment—frost-bitten fingertips festering, mucous membrane of nose gone, saliva glands of mouth refusing duty, skin coming off whole body'. I was not in good condition myself but nowhere near as debilitated as he had been.

Just how bad I was was still unknown to me although I was conscious that the crew had edged closer to my position to do the third medical and to gauge my feelings on being delayed again by weather. But Antarctica intervened with winds of such ferocity that their finding a way to my tent was soon out of the question. I spent another night fully dressed and fearful of tent failure, with the wind easing enough by the morning for me to see the crew's collection of tents and vehicles only a few hundred metres away.

The crew approached the next day during the lull in the weather, declaring their intention not to move anywhere, based on reports they had received that the storm would worsen and on the fact that one of their skidoos was not fully operational. They insisted that I too should stay put for my own safety. I was annoyed and told them as much, the cameras rolling as I did so. I had travelled in weather like this many times on my journey to the South Pole and it was a willingness to travel in such weather that had enabled me to get there so quickly on that occasion. Now they were laying down the law about whether or not I should travel. My whole world focused on knowing exactly what my routine was to be the next day, weather permitting, and the thought of possible delays was a great burden.

By that evening, the conditions had deteriorated to the extent that travel really was impossible. A steady supply of snow, threatening to cover my sleeping bag in drift, had started pouring in from the top of the tent through the large holes that had appeared near its apex as a result of the ill-fitting sled runners and skis having worn through the fabric. If I allowed the snow to keep coming in, it would soon cover me completely and, worse still, would melt, making the top of my sleeping bag as sodden as the bottom had long since become. By morning I would be knee deep in snow unless I did something immediately. The only thing for it was to fetch my large calico bag from the box on the sled and tie it into position over the apex. That meant going outside.

One of the most dangerous places to be in Antarctica, if statistics are to be believed, is just outside your tent in a zero-visibility blizzard. The number of people who have left their tent for whatever reason and become lost and disoriented, dying as a result of being unable to find their tent again, rivals the number of deaths by more seemingly dangerous means such as crevasse falls. So it was with some trepidation that I prepared to go outside. Tying one end of the spare rope round my waist and the other around the tent door, I plunged into the whiteness. It was an affront to all the senses: noisy, malevolent, biting cold, with snow and ice whipped up by the gale stinging my face. A rude awakening compared with the relative calm of the tent.

I tied the door shut behind me, testing that the rope was fast before moving away from the tent and taking tentative steps towards the area where I'd moored the sled the day before. After barely 2 metres, the tent had vanished, my lifeline disappearing into the mist behind me. I moved cautiously another couple of metres until I came across the sled, the mast the only thing protruding from the drift, and felt my way to the sled box, in which there was a large calico bag and a spare rope, which had been John's pulling rope. I grabbed them, resealed the box, and retraced my steps back along the rope to the tent. Easing the opening of the bag over the top of the tent, I pulled the draw string tight, securing it further with a hangman's noose made with John's old pulling rope. I attached the other end of the rope to the spade and pushed the blade deep into the ground upwind of the tent to help support it. By the time I got back into the tent I was frozen, my hands only just able to untie and retie the tent door, a deep numbness having set in. I pulled off my trousers and fell into the bag, thrusting my frozen hands between my thighs to warm them. To use Scott's words, it was indeed an awful place.

Other than unwelcome excursions outside the tent to sort out emergencies, blizzard days often involved extended periods of introspection. Among the multitude of thoughts that flitted across my mind were illogical fears of the storm never finishing and my being trapped here. Such thoughts made me marvel at how prisoners serving a life sentence and facing such a reality can keep themselves from going insane. Six days of inaction in the past eight were bad enough. To pass the time, I compared my journey with that of Mawson and Mertz, with further structure to my day provided by the endless succession of personal and equipment

Previous page: *An introspective moment during a day spent tent-bound;*
above: *Back to the future: Wade's camera incongruous amidst our 100-year-old gear.*

problems that needed to be resolved. Above all, though, the one thing I looked forward to was reading my daily diary, an 'anthology' compiled for me by my girlfriend, Elizabeth.

I drew comfort and inspiration from the diary in much the same way as Mawson had from the *Meditations* of Marcus Aurelius and letters from his fiancée, Paquita. *Meditations*, the recommended reading material of all upstanding Edwardian men, contains a series of observations distilled from the life experiences of the Roman general and emperor Marcus Aurelius, and is written in the form of a code of conduct to which one should adhere. I too had taken it with me to see what insights it provided but found it dry and stilted, its doctrine scant comfort compared with the compassion, personal insights and real emotions present in Elizabeth's anthology. This included some of her favourite poems together with personal messages for me for each day of my journey. The way in which her choice of words catered to my frame of mind at particular points of the journey was a source of continual amazement to me. Her ability to anticipate my moods, never having taken part in such an expedition, from her distant vantage point in west London and in a diary written months before I even began my journey, made me feel closer to her than she could possibly know. It showed to me both how well she knew me and the effort she had put into imagining where my mind might be at given points, and I loved her very dearly for it. I loved her very dearly anyway, the distance and separation of the trip having brought that home to me with blinding clarity. I determined, that day high up on the polar plateau, that when I returned I would ask her to marry me.

Mentally transporting oneself far away could, of course, be a double-edged sword, as it made returning to a lonely state back in the tent more of a shock to the system. For self-preservation I therefore found it best to keep part of my mind on my reality, regardless of where my imagination chose to escape to. The key was not to try to forget where I was but to look at the positives of my circumstances, to take one thing at a time and to put the whole experience into some kind of perspective.

All that said, that night I relished reading her anthology, leaving it to just before I turned in to do so and opening it on Day 30's entry in eager anticipation. The chosen poem was 'Say Not the Struggle Naught Availeth' by Arthur Clough. As I read the words, they reminded me that success was achievable if I could just keep body and soul together. Clough describes a battle scene, a wonderful metaphor for my circumstances:

> *If hopes were dupes, fears may be liars;*
> *It may be, in yon smoke concealed,*
> *Your comrades chase e'en now the fliers,*
> *And, but for you, possess the field.*

I remembered how all aspects of this project had been brought together against the odds: trying to get funding and support from broadcasters; organising the complex logistics; researching and sourcing all of the old gear, food and clothing. Now it really only remained for me to keep it together for just a couple of weeks longer. I took great solace from Clough's words 'But westward, look, the land is bright', and indeed it would be if I could just keep going.

An ongoing concern was how much food I had left. This I had calculated and recalculated many times, basing it on my taking two more weeks from this point to cover the remaining 140 kilometres of the journey. My tally was nine small bags of kangaroo jerky, five pieces of pemmican (each about the size of a mobile phone), thirty-two boiled sweets, six tea bags, twelve cubes of chocolate, some weak cocoa–powdered milk mix, some raisins and a small piece of butter. It was a miserly amount of food, but if I could just get half-decent conditions I stood a reasonable chance.

To cover the equivalent distance to Mawson, I knew I needed to climb higher into a headwind and colder temperatures for another week or so. The key was to keep in sight the incentive of the final section to the coast, which, in addition to being downhill, should involve tail winds and icy conditions where the sled might run better. If I could reach that point I could head for home, away from the plateau, in perhaps as little as a week.

Sometime during that night the wind abated, and Day 31 revealed the prospect of movement, snapping me out of any feelings of moroseness. Now more than ever I knew I had to focus on breaking down the forthcoming critical days and weeks into their component parts, working to achieve small milestones and keeping to my routine as best as I could in order to preserve both my dwindling food and reserves of strength.

Opposite: *The cramped conditions of the tent.*

I determined now to travel based on what the weather and my reduced energy levels allowed, even if that meant going on for a little longer on days when the weather was reasonable. This differed from how I'd operated until now, which had involved doing a certain amount each day and trying to maximise time spent in the tent resting and recuperating. The latter method, though good in theory, wasn't allowing me to cover the ground quickly enough, as it relied on a decent number of good weather days, which I just wasn't experiencing. With February nearly upon me, I knew the weather was only going to get worse.

8 Climbing

I pushed off into the teeth of the stiff downhill wind that has earned its own description—katabatic—with the uneven ground putting strain on my ankles, painful now from weeks of trudging in stiff leather and the bruising it had caused. The sun was up there somewhere, letting just enough diffuse light through to cast faint shadows on the sastrugi. With enough definition to see the lie of the land I could pick my route using the sastrugi's orientation as a natural pointer. . . .

The storms of the past week had stripped the sastrugi of all loose snow, leaving them deep and difficult to pull through: petrified standing waves with large troughs up to a metre deep in between. It was demoralising terrain through which to travel, sastrugi seemingly designed to stop the sled dead. The next few days of climbing seemed to take me through them at an awkward diagonal, corresponding to the direction from which the headwind was coming, adding to the difficulty. I knew I was approaching a crux point of the expedition.

Previous page: *The moon over the plateau felt as close as objects on the distant horizon.*

As I pulled, the sled rocked awkwardly from side to side as first one runner and then the other dropped into the valleys between the ridges of sastrugi, twisting the whole length of the sled as it went. Now that the sled was only half its starting length, the tent with the massive wooden frame stitched into it protruded and speared into the backs of the waves. Time after time it lunged into walls of ice, finally pushing one of the 'tent poles' straight through the top, tearing a massive hole. This would mean another emergency repair. In the meantime I positioned the tent further back on the sled to try to avoid the same thing happening again, having to put up instead with the back of the tent now catching the tops of sastrugi and acting like a brake.

I set myself goals and focused my mind on trying to reach pieces of ice several hundred metres away or get through the next short block of time. Any thoughts of the conditions improving or the greater whole were inconceivable and unproductive in equal measure. Taking inspiration from Mawson's attitude to do his 'utmost to the last', I just chipped away at the total while seldom giving its overall achievement much serious consideration.

When my thoughts did drift to what would happen if I actually made it, they deflated rather than encouraged me. Such thinking was dangerous for a couple of reasons. First, because any thoughts of this were premature in the extreme given all the things that could still go wrong; second, because considering the end-game meant thinking through the possible consequences of my success. I wondered whether the trip would attract criticism because I had not eaten dog livers or had anyone die on me, somehow invalidating what I had done. If I were claiming to have achieved the same as Mawson, this would of course be true, but I was not. I would have got as close as was possible to Mawson's experience, in the knowledge that he had suffered far worse and achieved far more than I had.

However, I hadn't had the benefit of dogs to help pull my sled for the first two weeks as Mawson had had, instead having to carry my substitute dog-meat from the outset, and, due to the circular nature of my route, I did not have the benefit of the tail winds that he had had either. I gave the internal debate a rest, pulled myself together and focused on the next steps.

Previous page: *Alone on the plateau;*
opposite: *The lull after the storm. A calm day, with my balaclava rolled up to stop overheating.*

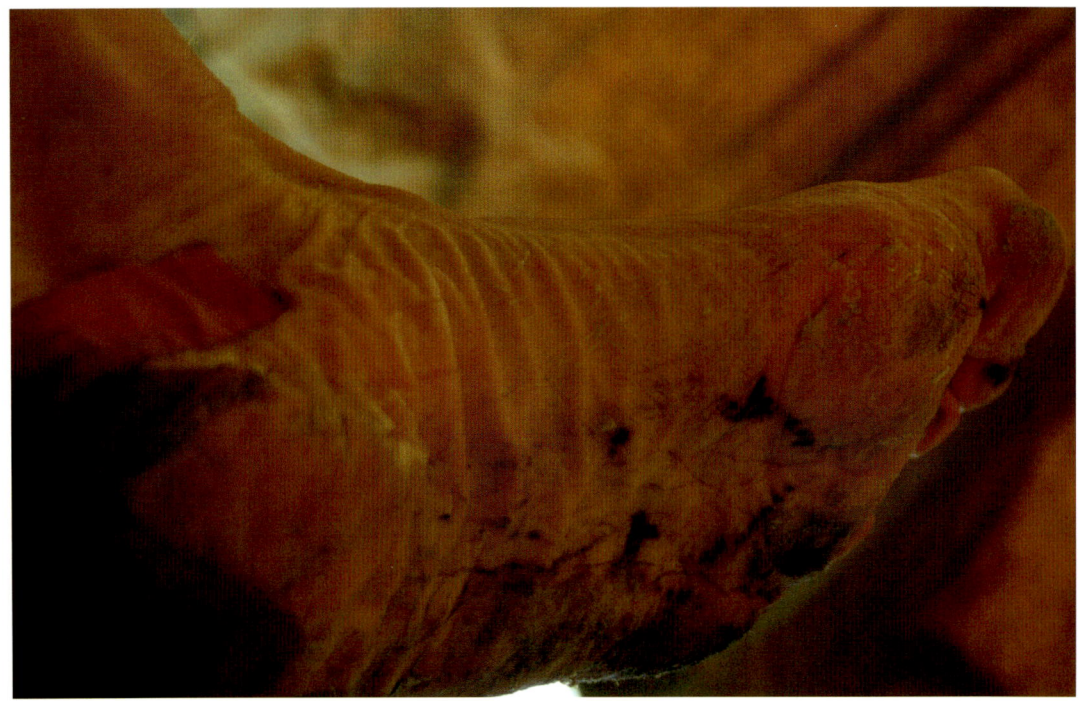

Mawson was slowing down dramatically by this point in his journey because of the terrible state of his feet and the unusually warm temperatures. 'Almost all descent but the surface cut my feet up', he noted. The temperatures were so warm that the snow and ice surface were actually melting, with 'running water in later afternoon . . . all I could do to pull the sledge downhill'. By Day 36 the 'surface became more deep in snow and sun softened it although wind very good later'. At this point I had begun to get ahead of Mawson for the first time. While he was descending, I was ascending to colder, higher ground to match the amount of climbing he had done. He ascended later and had a colder run, but for now relative warmth and wetness were his problems, just as they had been for Mertz much of the time.

I finally pitched the tent after a hard day's climbing, intrigued to see how well it now blended in with its surroundings—its beige fabric had been bleached by the blistering ultraviolet radiation of Antarctica to a dirty off-white. This was a legacy of the enormous amount of

Above: *The skin damage on the base of my foot.*

radiation that reaches ground level, much of it due to the hole in the Earth's protective ozone layer caused by humans' release of chlorofluorocarbons (CFCs), which destroy ozone, into the atmosphere. Although the use of CFCs has been phased out since 1987 with the signing of a multilateral agreement, the effects of this pollution still wreak havoc in Antarctica. This happens predominantly in the winter when Antarctica's air mass becomes isolated from the rest of the world's weather, allowing wide-scale ozone destruction to occur. Generally speaking, the hole has been reducing in size since its worst excesses of the 1980s and 1990s, but it is still bigger each winter than the Antarctic continent itself, or twice the size of Australia, with little or nothing shielding the place from the full force of the sun's rays.

The ultraviolet radiation that ravages Antarctica by day is at least gone by evening. As the sun dropped low on the horizon that night, it produced one of the most beautiful sunsets I had ever seen. I could see clear to the horizon across a seemingly limitless sea of grey and white icy chop. An eerie silence came with the stillness that night, the sun's crimson rays becoming longer and weaker as darkness gradually descended over the ice. Momentarily distracted with my work, when I looked up again a wonderful vertical shaft of light had appeared, emanating from the top of the sun and going straight up to the heavens: a magical solar pillar. The low temperatures in Antarctica normally mean that little or no water vapour is held in the air; instead, it freezes and falls out. But that night the air sparkled, full of small ice particles reflecting the dying rays of the sun to form this strange phenomenon that I had not seen before. I was alone with the sound of my footfalls, heavy breathing and the austere beauty of this place, which so often I was too preoccupied to appreciate. I suspected that, ironically, when this was all over, I would look back fondly at my time here alone with the immensity of nature, totally insignificant in the grand scheme of things. In that moment, I did not want the trip to end or to have to return to the modern world. It was fifteen minutes before the cold finally forced me to seek the shelter of the tent.

My cold tolerance had reduced in the past days, a combination of colder conditions and my loss of body weight. My legs, even though I scarcely saw them unclothed, had reduced in size; my woollen thermals were loose now, the fabric rucked up in folds where before it had been skin-tight. My right foot was a problem, and in particular the big and second toes, which had turned white and had been completely without sensation for more than a week. The skin on the soles of both feet was black and shrivelled in many places.

I had begun a program of warming the toes on my right foot to try to ensure that frostbite did not develop. This involved heating water to within a couple of minutes of boiling and then, crouching awkwardly in the tent, my head touching the ceiling, immersing my foot in it. Even though the scalding water left a red tidemark on my foot I felt no sensation, and there was no colour change to the two problem toes. I just hoped it was nerve damage and nothing worse.

On Day 32 I was sheltered behind the sled, like a limpet on a rock, the wind doing its best to displace me. I had been too tired to do anything but concentrate on taking one step at a time, in the knowledge that the kilometres would pass beneath me despite the lack of any visual evidence to support the fact. I had already eaten my hooch meal that morning with a little bit of butter that I'd been saving, and had endured a gut-wrenching climb of 9 kilometres uphill into a fierce headwind of 45 kilometres an hour. Four more days of this and all my climbing should be done: I could finally turn for the coast, warmer conditions and ultimately rest.

Previous page: *A solar pillar, caused by the dying rays of the sun refracting through airborne ice crystals;* above, left to right: *The top of the Haggelund provides a different view of the plateau; Wade silhouetted against a crimson sky; a warm day and some human contact—being interviewed by the crew.*

My mood was fragile. It took surprisingly little to turn my mental state from positive to negative. As I sheltered behind the sled, a full cup of cocoa slipped out of my mitted hand, its warm contents vanishing into the ice below me. I swore loudly and copiously, turning the ice around me to new shades of blue, and spent the next hour persuading myself that this minor event was just that. And that was the problem: there was no point of reference to enable me to put its loss into any kind of perspective. Antarctica just looked on dispassionately.

On Day 33 I had my third medical. I didn't relish the prospect of finding out my weight, particularly with its implications for the continuation of my journey. I had not defecated for six days and although I had been feeling the need since the previous day, I was so worried about my low weight and its working against me that I held back. At this point I felt that every gram counted.

The medical was a very cold experience, as the modern polar pyramid tent in which it was conducted could not be warmed without compromising the operation of the camera. Warmth meant condensation and a fogged lens, and that was not good for filming. The temperature was a couple of degrees above zero at best, making it difficult for me to keep myself warm as I sat there being prodded and poked.

I couldn't absolve myself from some of the responsibility for the medicals. They had been developed with Mawson's old university—Adelaide—and its medical department months before, and I had consented to them at the time. They involved skin-fold tests at predetermined points on the body, weight measurement and the taking of blood and urine samples. The data was then measured against my baseline level of health established through an exhaustive series of tests back in Adelaide, to determine both short-term and longer term physical deterioration caused by starvation and exposure to the cold. The baseline tests had included CAT scans to measure heart and lung capacity and muscularity, DEXA body-mass scans, a series of blood and urine tests and the wearing of 'accelerometers' designed to measure total body movement. The accelerometer data, considered in conjunction with my weight loss and the food I had consumed, enabled a calculation of how efficiently my body converted food into energy.

Blood was taken from vessels that were tight and constricted by the cold, while the doctor casually posed questions about my bodily functions and the state of my extremities as I tried to remain warm. I volunteered that I had defecated only four times in the whole trip but made sure I didn't mention the problems with the toes on my right foot.

Interestingly, the conclusion was that I'd lost only a couple of kilograms since my last medical, conducted ten or so days before. I was quietly ecstatic, as it meant that for now at least I was safe from being stopped on medical grounds, and that I was travelling as efficiently as I could given the circumstances, having slowed the slide towards 25 kilograms of weight loss. The atmosphere in the medical tent was distinctly anticlimactic, reminiscent of the immediate moments after the downgrade of a serious emergency to a routine drill. It wasn't that people wanted me to fail, rather that a more dramatic weight loss was anticipated. I wasn't about to oblige. One day I knew this trip would be over, 'but not yet, not today', I thought to myself.

The seed was sown in my mind and I wondered whether I was in some way doing it easy compared with Mawson. I dwelt on this latest distraction for some time as I trudged off into the biting headwind. Was my 18 kilograms of weight loss really an indicator of how hard I had tried and a measure of how much less I had suffered? I wasn't sure. I lined up the compass on a piece of ice on the distant horizon and walked away from the medical tent, the plateau at least representing a known quantity against which I could pit myself.

Opposite: *At least the flag is flying proudly.*

The wind was gusting heavily, as usual. It posed problems by making me colder and providing resistance to pulling the sled, and caused the snow to billow around and settle on my clothes, melting as it did so. Really I needed neither strong tail winds nor strong headwinds: just less wind full stop. My definition of light wind since being out here meant 30 to 40 kilometres per hour.

Mawson was just about to experience the most serious event since Mertz's death. It was Day 34 and he described the conditions: 'Light extremely bad and only by great strain on eyes could I keep a course. I escaped several large open crevasses by Providence not seeing them until past them . . . I blundered blindly on'. This was only the third time that Mawson had used the word 'Providence' in a diary that is otherwise functional and pragmatic, devoted to recording progress, problems encountered and solved and the general logistics of expedition life for him and Mertz: the product of a controlled, Edwardian, scientific mind.

On Day 35 Mawson's worst fears about crevasses came true. As he climbed through deep snow, a snow bridge over an invisible crevasse collapsed under his weight.

> *A few moments later I was dangling on end of rope in crevasse, sledge creeping to mouth expecting every moment the sledge to crash on my head and both of us to go to the bottom unseen below. Then I thought of the food left uneaten in the sledge—and, as the sledge stopped without coming down, I thought of Providence again giving me a chance. The chance looked very small as the rope had sawed into the overhanging lid, my finger ends all damaged, myself weak . . . with the feeling that Providence was helping me I made a great struggle, half getting out then skipping back again several times but at last just did it. Then I felt grateful to Providence . . . I trust to Providence who has so many times already helped me.*

Providence, for Mawson, was now an active aid. It is clear from the language he used that it was more than a synonym for fate. His continued allusions to a spiritual benefactor are increasingly removed from the dry science of his early diary entries.

Previous page: *Wade using the Haggelund as a good vantage point as I appear out of the vastness;* opposite: *Grim determination, even though the wind has dropped and pulling is easier today.*

Mawson's Crevasse Fall

On Day 35 Mawson fell through a weak snow bridge over an invisible crevasse, his pulling rope the only thing preventing him plunging to his death in the depths of the chasm over which he subsequently hung. He was at the end of his tether, both literally and metaphorically. In his diary, he later described his initial thoughts, how close he had been to just letting go to end all the pain and suffering: 'So this is the end'. Several years later, in *The Home of the Blizzard*, he expanded on what he had been thinking at the time: 'There on the brink of the great Beyond I well remember how I looked forward to the peace of the great release —how almost excited I was at the prospect of the unknown to be unveiled'.

The food left behind on the sled, ironically, provided incentive for him to get out and keep going, according to him, more so than more philosophical thoughts of loved ones back home, public expectation, the memory of Ninnis and Mertz, or a sense of duty. This is not as unusual as it might appear: it is my belief that these were all inextricably linked for Mawson. It somehow would not sit well with him and his organised approach to things if, suspecting as he now did that he could make it to the hut with the available food, he allowed himself the ignominy of dying by falling into a crevasse. It somehow flew in the face of his scientific discipline and his belief that Providence wanted him to make it by again giving him a chance. It was a test. If he failed he would have failed on multiple counts: the expedition would have failed, his disciplined approach would have come up short, his scientific findings would have been lost and he would have let 'Providence' down despite being given multiple chances. By surviving he would be vindicated and could snatch victory from the jaws of defeat on all counts. To his mind it was the only outcome for the expedition and the poor situation in which he found himself. And so, galvanised as he was, he clawed his way more than 4 metres to the lip of the crevasse, cold, alone, hungry and with failing strength, mouthing the words of Service's poem to himself like a mantra as he went: 'Just have one more try—it's dead easy to die / It's the keeping-on-living that's hard'. After several desperate attempts, he finally appeared on the surface, so exhausted that he fell asleep on the snow, waking an hour later to put up the tent and fall in to his sleeping bag.

Later, in *Home of the Blizzard*, Mawson recorded in an unusually pensive frame of mind: 'the mood o

the Persian philosopher appealed to me: "Unborn tomorrow and dead yesterday, why fret about them if today be sweet'". It was at that moment he decided to eat his remaining food at a faster rate to give himself the strength to make it to the hut more quickly, rather than risk falling into another crevasse leaving food uneaten on the sled and the

prospect of insufficient strength to pull himself out again. He also took the precaution of fabricating a primitive rope ladder out of his pulling rope to improve his chances of getting out. Whatever assistance Providence promised, Mawson the pragmatist wasn't going to leave any more to chance than he needed to.

After hard days of pulling uphill for the most part, my Day 36 finally brought my last period of climbing south-west, with only 17 kilometres more of ascent before I could finally turn my back on the plateau and head instead for the coast. I was relieved to be making for lower ground with the wind at my back at last; the sense of having turned the final corner gave me a real boost. It was, ironically, relatively calm in the evening when I made camp, after having spent four hours pulling in high wind. I would have waited for a slight lessening of the wind had I known it was coming, as Antarctica has a good sixteen or eighteen hours of daylight at that time of the year.

Even though the bindings from the skis had fallen victim to one of my weight-saving purges a few weeks earlier, their rubbing against the fabric of the tent beforehand had caused wear that was now beginning to show badly. This, combined with the wind and damage from ultraviolet radiation, meant that both the top and sides of the tent had holes open to the elements, with my large calico bag no longer large enough to cover the gaping hole at the top. But, after hauling all day in the icy conditions, my hands were too cold for me to think about making an extensive repair to the tent from the outside, so I did what I could from the inside, half in my sleeping bag.

Above left: *Alone with my thoughts, but still being 'followed' by the sled;*
above right: *The crew's camp, with the Haggelund at left.*

That night I woke at 2 a.m. to find that, because the rip in the tent had grown, I could now make out the night sky complete with a smattering of stars through the hole. I was shocked by just how dark it was. Darkness tends to be something that few polar explorers experience out on the ice, as Antarctic journeys are undertaken in the summer, when all waking hours are light and the temperatures more bearable. Winter Antarctic travel is something to be avoided at all costs, as the temperatures then are difficult to survive.

Perhaps the most infamous winter-time Antarctic journey was that of Apsley Cherry-Garrard, Henry 'Birdie' Bowers and Dr Edward Wilson while they were on Robert Scott's Terra Nova Expedition of June 1911. It was a journey of necessity rather than design, after a blizzard destroyed their tent and scattered their provisions. Cherry-Garrard's account of their journey through the bitter cold and inky darkness of the Antarctic winter over obstructive icy terrain is unambiguously titled *The Worst Journey in the World*. The men had an epic struggle to save themselves. All three narrowly survived, but only Cherry-Garrard returned home from Antarctica: Bowers and Wilson died tragically with Scott the following summer out on the Ross Ice Shelf, only 20 kilometres from a food cache that would have saved them.

With each day now bringing with it a longer night, I felt a sense of urgency to get moving as quickly as I could and reach the coast and safety.

9 Iceberg Alley

I woke to a day that, just to confuse matters, was the warmest yet. The temperature in the tent was a balmy zero with the sun on the canvas. I was dog-tired but had slept well that night in the knowledge that the wind could blow as hard as it liked since I was on my downhill leg towards the coast and home. As if confirmation were needed, the compass needle pointed in the direction I knew I was now headed for the first time—north.

Stepping into the harness, I pulled for an hour through undulating terrain until I reached a point at the top of a perceptible rise where, for perhaps only the second or third time during the whole journey, I was immediately aware of a more distant horizon—an indication of the great height I was now at. Although the coast would not be visible for some days, I was energised to know that it was down there. Heading for it now was just the tonic I needed.

It was several hours before the descent actually felt like one, as the snow was too warm and soft to pull through easily. I was sinking through up to my ankles, 10 centimetres or so—enough

Previous page: *Trudging across the slope in the relative warmth of the coast.*

to be energy sapping. The sled didn't run well either; the effects of waxing the runners several weeks before had long since worn off, and the wet snow was clinging to them enthusiastically, creating considerable drag. It was like pulling through treacle. In the end I just ran out of steam, getting dehydrated in the blazing sun. I had to take off my Burberry, jumper, balaclava and mitts to try to reduce heat in the intense ultraviolet radiation of these southern latitudes. I called it a day having covered about 18 kilometres, which I thought was excellent going, considering the conditions.

Above: *The undulating landscape closer to the coast.*

That night I had a raging thirst, having not drunk enough during the day. My one thermos held only a litre of water and nowhere near enough for the effort I was putting in. If tiredness and lack of food hadn't restricted my days to only four or five hours of pulling, dehydration soon would have. I gunned the stove for almost three hours to melt enough snow to sate my thirst. As I waited for the snow to melt, I found myself contemplating when all this snow surrounding me might have fallen. Here at the coast snowfall was frequent, but in many parts of the interior it was not, much of it having fallen between hundreds and hundreds of thousands of years before, making Antarctica the driest continent on earth.

Incredible, then, that the continent is made up of such a massive expanse of ice. Twice the size of Australia, the ice cap has an average thickness of more than 2 kilometres—a staggering 28 million cubic kilometres of the stuff, representing 90 per cent of the world's fresh water. I drank my fill of precious 'fossil water', turned off the stove and lay back in the sleeping bag to sleep.

Given how much water is locked up in the ice of this place, it concerned me that I should be experiencing 'warm' conditions, although Mawson recorded not dissimilar conditions himself. He noted in his diary that 'the sun came out so warm that the rough ice surface underfoot was covered with a film of water and in some places small trickles ran away to disappear into crevasses' and that 'though the course was downhill, the sledge required a good deal of pulling owing to the wet runners'. After my day of hauling, I certainly sympathised with his experience with the runners.

I had looked forward to moving downhill to the coast for so long, using it as an incentive to keep me going when things were desperate. But now that I was experiencing this downhill section, it was not as easy as I had hoped. I had a good tail wind at my back but, in addition to the wet and heavy snow, the sastrugi were larger, due to the stronger wind, and the tent 'prow' continually snagged on their backs.

The next morning, mindful of the difficulties of the day before, I refocused on small goals, thinking only of making it to my first break in an hour's time, where a boiled sweet, a few raisins and a slug of icy water awaited. Thinking of finishing was too dangerous a game to play. The journey would not be over until I had taken the last step, and I still had 60 kilometres to go. In this place that stripped life back to the basic elements of light, warmth, shelter, food and water, much of my mental energy was taken up solving issues and ensuring they didn't become magnified out of all proportion. Humans have the capacity, varying from person to person, for a certain amount of worry or anxiety in their lives. It is part of my philosophy to ensure that this finite amount of 'life stress' is associated with achieving something worthwhile, and Antarctic trips are the embodiment of this for me. Now, my very proximity to the end had begun to exert some friendly pressure of its own, with fears about an ankle sprain, crevasse fall, frostbite or serious blizzard preying on my mind.

On the other hand, there was something fantastically exciting about perceptibly descending off the vast Antarctic ice cap towards the sea on foot. To have covered so much ground and now be walking my way to the end of such a gruelling journey under my own steam was exhilarating—I had had the same buzz with each of my three previous polar journeys. Unlike the previous day, I was moving quickly now with the wind assisting me. There was no need for the sail as the sled presented enough of a surface area for the wind to catch.

Moving northwards, although more slowly than me, was the very ground I walked on—the ice cap itself. In some places, it moves a few hundred metres northwards each year, towards the ocean. I wondered what this meant for Ninnis and Mertz, whose bodies had been interred in the ice within weeks of one another ninety-five years before. For Ninnis, who fell into a crevasse on the glacier that now bears his name, his body and the ice surrounding it would likely have broken off into the ocean years ago, given the speed at which glaciers move. Even for Mertz, who died on the plateau between the Ninnis and Mertz glaciers, a few hundred metres a year over the course of almost a century would have moved him perhaps 20 kilometres towards the sea, making his final resting place the frigid Southern Ocean. It seems that even in death humans cannot establish a permanent presence on Antarctica.

I sat on the sled for a break, the wind at my back, squinting towards the horizon and trying to work out what I was seeing—a flat line several centimetres across and raised above the level of the distant horizon. It wasn't exactly on the bearing I wanted to follow but, if I kept it out to my right, it was a good point of reference. The penny dropped and my pulse quickened: it was barely visible but it had to be an iceberg out in the ocean. I checked the compass, standing on the sled to give myself more height. It was an iceberg. I quickly stepped back into the harness

and moved off with childlike excitement towards what in the final analysis was just another piece of ice. But unlike the small pieces of sastrugi I had navigated towards throughout the journey, this was a massive expanse, its visible cliffs, hundreds of metres high, representing a mere 10 per cent of its total size.

I spent ages wondering about the iceberg, enjoying the stimulation of something new to consider as, over the course of the following hours, it gradually revealed more of itself. By day's end it was still far off but I could see it was indeed flat, as if drawn with a ruler. It was

Above: *Wearing fewer clothes means more to tie on the sled.*

reminiscent of the flat table-topped mountains I had seen when trekking through Australia's deserts—mesas or buttes to use their correct terms. It was still too far away to say for sure but the fact that it was flat meant that it was likely a new berg from the cap, rather than one of the more angular icebergs, complete with jagged crevassing, that calve off glaciers or one of the old bergs that 'rot' as their ice melts with the action of the sea and sun.

My enthusiasm on seeing the berg and barrelling towards it was soon tempered by lack of fuel in the tank as my legs began to weaken and my mood deflate. I did not need to be reminded that I was down to very small amounts of food. That night in the tent I laid it all out in front of me. Three daily portions of ground-up kangaroo jerky and three small bags of meat jerky, a cup of sugar, no sweets, a small amount of butter, six biscuits, three tea bags and my last piece of pemmican. This very small larder would give me food for three more days at most for the remaining 40 kilometres of travel and the nightmarish prospect of extricating myself from a crevasse.

The ground around me was now mostly half blue ice interspersed with thin drifts of snow perhaps 30 centimetres deep. This had made it hard to find a decent place to pitch the tent that night, as I needed snow into which to knock my crude pegs and to dig blocks thick enough to weigh down the valances.

I hoped the weather would hold. One more three-day blizzard would still finish me off with the small amount of food I had left, and the wind that accompanied such a storm would test the shallow purchase of the pegs and the small snow blocks I had been able to chip out of the icy ground. I hoped that, as the ground became more and more icy tomorrow as I descended further, I would actually be able to find enough snow on which to pitch the tent and to melt for water to drink.

Mawson, on the other hand, seemed to be experience soft snow in his final week, with falling snow and 'surface deep snow' both featuring in his accounts. On Day 41, the snow was so deep that 'very little sastrugi traces as surface about here appears very flat and deep softish

Previous page: *The birthplace of icebergs: tabular icebergs clog the sea;*
opposite: *A skua circling, looking for food or perhaps just company.*

snow'. To compensate for his workload he continued to discard items: 'I throw away my crampons and the alpine rope and crevasse stick tonight'. The prospect of a successful end to his struggle was still far from his mind.

I woke to a sunny but windy day with more bergs revealing themselves in the first hours of travel, like ships' masts on the horizon with hulls not yet having appeared. I continued to descend towards the coast and, although the sea was still not visible, a shadow appeared on the ground next to me, revealing a skua circling above, patiently checking me out. As skuas obtain almost 90 per cent of their food from penguin eggs, and all penguins live within a short distance of the coast, I realised the ocean must be very near now. All animals, birds included, seldom stray far from a thin ribbon around the coast in Antarctica, as most of the continent is a frigid, high-altitude desert. Quite what he was doing up here then I wasn't sure. I doubted it was for my company—more likely he was wondering if I, or anything on my sled, were edible. One thing was for sure; we were the only ones stupid enough to be up here, some 15 kilometres from the sea.

The strong tail wind combined with the downward gradient on blue ice meant the sled moved up alongside me, such that I now walked parallel with it—as a stable-hand would walk a horse—holding the towing rope lightly like reins rather than pulling. Occasional gusts even pushed the sled ahead of me with such force that I had to dig in with my hobnails and brace myself to avoid being pulled off my feet. This was a new experience.

The day before I had lost the heel of one of my hobnail boots due to the strain I was putting on it, trying to keep my balance. The heel must have become stuck in the ice, for when I took my boots off at the end of the day all that was left on my right boot was a stump of leather, which made walking more uneven and dicey on the polished turquoise ice. Partly because I had lost my heel and partly to test Mawson's technology, I decided to don my replica wooden crampons to negotiate the lethally slippery, and increasingly steep, ice. I had carried them from the start. They were made from old packing-case wood, with nails and screws protruding from them to give me grip on the ice, and were an exact copy of Mawson's. He had discarded his crampons only days previously and then found he needed them for his final descent to the coast from Aladdin's Cave, through precisely the kind of terrain I now found myself on. I could see why.

The slope became steeper but the crampons provided just enough grip to enable me to descend. I let the sled run ahead of me as I went. The dark of the ocean now stretched ahead of me, complete with dozens of brilliant white icebergs stretching into the distance like a white armada. Some small rocks had also begun to appear out on my left, their dark brown contrasting with the white of the snow and ice. I chuckled to myself as a further hour's travel towards them in fact revealed them to be the large weathered peaks of the Vestfold Hillss, exposed with the retreat of the ice cap. Antarctica had played its normal tricks by depriving me of any point of reference by which to judge their size. It seemed like an eternity ago that I was last up on the Skiway, 30 or so kilometres from here, at the beginning of this epic journey.

Only hours before I had had genuine fears of not being able to find sufficient snow to pitch the tent and having to wrap myself in my sleeping bag inside the tent cover and spend the night in the open. Now these fears appeared to be unfounded, as I found myself emerging from the blue ice surface into fields of thick snow in the lee of the Vestfolds.

I descended further, the slope steepening as I went until it was close to 40 degrees, appearing to head towards the edge of a precipice that as yet remained unseen. The sled had a mind of its own, and I feared that if the towing rope for any reason parted company with it, the sled and all my belongings would clatter down over the precipice to whatever lay below.

Suddenly there was a massive weight on the rope and the sled disappeared, doing exactly what I had just feared. I struggled to stay on my feet, slipping towards whatever drop it was that the sled hung over, conscious now that it must be hanging in space. Adrenaline surged as I pulled with all my might to lift the sled, hand over hand, protesting, back up onto the snow. This done, I then leaned into the harness and pulled the sled up the slope as far away from the drop as my strength allowed before dropping to the snow, panting with exertion. Ironic that the film crew were not here to film real drama as it unfolded, I thought to myself.

Traversing the slope diagonally away from the drop with sled safely in tow, I saw what it was I had almost stumbled over: a 30-metre ice cliff that would surely have caused me serious injury or worse had I gone over it. With the adrenaline, I had had neither the time nor energy to panic, and now thankfully it was behind me.

Finally, reaching more level ground at the toe of the adjacent slope, I made camp, exhausted after a day made much longer by my quest for the flat ground I needed for the tent. I was just glad to be down. Tomorrow would herald new challenges, including finding a way back out of the bowl in which I now found myself and covering the remaining 20 kilometres of my journey. The film crew would also require me to extricate myself from a crevasse as Mawson had done, as a 'controlled experiment'. Given how difficult it had been to pull up the sled an hour before, I wondered if I would have the strength to lift myself vertically out of an icy chasm. The end was in sight but it still seemed far, far away.

10 'Just Have One More Try— It's Dead Easy to Die'

I woke with a mixture of emotions: on the one hand, a feeling of intense satisfaction at almost having covered the same distance as Mawson and, on the other, a strange detachment brought on by my policy of flatly refusing to consider the achievement of the whole until it was done. The goal, even at this the eleventh hour, was instead a series of smaller milestones, the sum of which would lead to the completion of the journey. My approach tended to steal away the elation I should have felt at what had been achieved so far but it had kept me sane along the way when the total was too much to consider. . . .

The immediate goal was a steep diagonal climb of a couple of kilometres across the slope I had descended the night before. Once at the top of this, I would have 18 more kilometres of ground to cover to match Mawson's total distance.

After ninety minutes, I finally reached the top, stopping to rest on a conveniently positioned rock. I was hot from the exertion despite having left earlier in the morning than usual, in a bid to avoid the warmth and enjoy firmer snow conditions. I was unaccustomed to the balmy

Previous page: *Overheating in a land of ice*.

temperatures of a couple of degrees below zero down here on the coast, 1000 metres lower than where I had spent much of the past month and a half.

My seat was amidst rocky rubble: unfamiliar earthy hues after six weeks of blue and white. I sat at something of a crossroads: the amazing assortment of weathered pebbles surrounding me were brought here from the south by Antarctica's ice cap, not only worn smooth but dredged up and carried by it from distant subterranean places beneath the ice. Had I looked to the north 120 million years ago, India would have been visible just a couple of kilometres away, joined here as part of the super-continent Gondwanaland, before it broke loose and drifted north to collide with Asia and form the Himalaya.

Far below me lurked the cliff over which I had almost fallen the day before—the unnerving memory was not yet behind me. Beneath me I could hear subterranean running water, snowmelt from the warmth of the sun on the rocks.

I lifted my tired body again and moved off. Several kilometres away the coast curved inland in a large bay, home to the icebergs I had seen the day before. No two bergs were the same, in either shape or hue. The colours ranged from turquoise and emerald green to grey and white, the variations caused by the different pressures that the ice had been subjected to, and beautiful beyond belief. My route took me within 500 metres of the icy shore, the snow soft beneath my feet as the sun rose higher. I removed layers to regulate body temperature, eventually down to just boots, woollen long johns and goggles.

I had been exposed to Antarctica's austere beauty for so long that it took me a while to wake up to what I was seeing: the remarkable jigsaw patterns of ice crystals that had formed on the ocean's surface and the icebergs themselves, massive, ephemeral lost worlds cast adrift in the ocean. The latter begin 'dying' as soon as they are born, melting and giving up the water that was locked in them thousands of years ago.

After several hours of hard work on my spectacular route parallel to the coast, I saw something completely incongruous on the horizon: several vehicles, belonging to the film crew. My 'Commonwealth Bay', and the endpoint of my journey, was there at the edge of the ocean near the vehicles, where quite literally one could go no further without plunging over cliffs

down to the icy fjord below. I stopped to rest for a moment and to try and comprehend what I had been through, watching the figures near the vehicles busying themselves, the brooding mountains a massive backdrop to the unlikely scene.

Mawson first sighted Commonwealth Bay on Day 46, a few days later than the point at which I now found myself, when dark 'water-sky' and not vehicles had appeared on the north-west horizon, indicating the sea. The next day, in 'thick weather' and with only a kilogram of food remaining, he stumbled into a small hummock of snow (a 'cairn') built by Archibald McLean, Alfred Hodgeman and Frank Hurley, who had been out searching for his party. They had

Above: *The brooding Vestfold Hills: from here, India would have been visible 120 million years ago.*

left a note that told Mawson the bearing and distance to Aladdin's Cave (the snow cave less than 16 kilometres from his hut) and gave news of his ship the *Aurora* having arrived and of men waiting at the hut.

More importantly, the searchers had left food. Although he had to wait a further ten days for human company, and no one yet knew of his fate or the events that had unfolded, Mawson had been saved. He knew people were waiting for him, and that he had to cover only 48 kilometres, with plentiful food and the prospect of more of it at Aladdin's Cave halfway to the hut.

The camera crew could see me coming. They knew to expect me: there was, of course, no one else walking down from the extremes of the plateau. The biggest surprise—to me at least—was the fact that I was here at all and that now, barring mishap, I would make it. I walked to the cliff's edge—ahead of me to the north only ocean—cast down the harness and sat heavily on the sled.

The end of Mawson's journey was quite different. The searchers would not have been expecting a knock at the door. They must have been astounded when the wreck of the human that was

Above left: *The crew carefully descend a snow slope to film my crevasse escape;*
above right: *Adjusting my makeshift wooden crampons, made from packing cases and nails, for a dicey descent down blue ice;*
opposite: *Tired but victorious.*

Mawson stumbled into the hut. Their question 'Which one are you?' speaks volumes. The less dramatic question with which I was greeted by the crew was 'How do you feel?'. I wasn't sure. I was exhausted and exhilarated in equal measure. I had gained a real appreciation of the painful magnitude of some of the difficult decisions that Mawson had to make and of how hard he had pushed himself but, other than that, there was too much information to process based on experiences that were still too raw. Impatiently, they pressed me again. How was I? What had I missed most? What did I now feel about Mawson the man and his achievement? The best I could offer was an unenlightening 'My God, what an effort'. It didn't scratch the surface of what it had been like but was all I could muster.

In fact, other than the feeling of indescribable relief and happiness at having finished, the moment, as sweet as it was, was strangely anticlimactic. The crew congratulated me, although the words did not really get through. The gratitude at finally being able to stop, however, was real. I was weak, I was desperately hungry, I missed the camaraderie of friends and family, and I longed for a return to normal life. My somewhat subdued mood was also due in no small part to having still one more hurdle to overcome after one final night under canvas—climbing out of Mawson's crevasse.

Climbing up a rope hand over hand is extremely difficult. It is exhausting: your arms fill with lactic acid, stopping the biceps from working and the fingers from gripping, and there is, of course, little chance of rest. But after almost a month and a half on the ice on starvation rations, I had willingly agreed to hang on the end of a rope inside a crevasse and do just that.

We had decided to attempt the crevasse exercise early in the morning in order to have colder, safer conditions, before the afternoon sun thawed snow bridges, making them weaker and less stable to cross. We found an area of obvious crevassing, where ice tumbled over the edge of the cliffs towards the sea below, and we were almost upon our chosen crevasse before it revealed itself: an innocuous enough crack of 20 centimetres on the surface that expanded from its neck to become 3 metres wide within a short distance of the surface.

Previous page: A lone figure on the edge of the ocean. The end of the road;
opposite: The Rusky keeps an eye on proceedings from a precarious position of his own over the crevasse.

As I was lowered in on a modern rope, I looked down between my feet and could see 10 or 15 metres beneath me. There the void narrowed to a jagged opening of only a metre or so across, and beyond this the chasm continued into penetrating cold and ominous dark. I thought briefly of Ninnis. It was a far bigger crevasse than this that had claimed him; what a desperate place to die it must have been.

Above left: *Trying to gain a foothold as I ascend the rope;*
above right: *On a ledge before descending into the crevasse proper.*

Shouts from above gave me warning as a length of old hemp rope appeared next to me, knots pre-tied in it at 40-centimetre intervals. The faces at the lip of the crevasse seemed a long way up as I steeled myself for the effort, kicking away a few icicles to give me a clearer path to the surface.

The camera rolled and I threw myself into the task. I had a vague plan to pull myself up the first metre or so and then, with enough slack rope hanging below me, to try to get my hobnailed boots onto either side of one of the bulbous knots. Then I could perhaps pause for long enough to lift again with my arms. The initial effort had me breathing heavily almost immediately as I crept up the rope. The problem came with trying to get a purchase with my feet as, hanging in space, I began to spin with my exertions. Being too far from the walls of the crevasse to steady myself I found it exceptionally difficult to balance, the metal hobnail studs catching awkwardly on the fibrous texture of the heavy hemp rope. Frantically I shook the rope clear of my boots, all my weight on my arms as I did so, managing after 10 seconds to get clear of it and move a further metre up the rope. My head was still almost 2 metres from the surface and I was tiring rapidly, and breathing hard.

I felt I had enough energy for only one more effort to get high enough up the rope to find a foothold near to the entrance of the crevasse. I threw myself upward again with a mighty effort, mindful now of keeping my feet clear of the rope. I thrust my left leg out and caught the hobnails on the toe of my boot on a small lip on the vertical wall. My foot held long enough for me to steady myself and turn through 180 degrees, repeating the exercise with my right foot, getting a better foothold. With a frenzied push with my legs and a last weakening pull with my arms, I emerged on my stomach onto the snow, spreading my weight as best I could to ensure I didn't break through the lip of the crevasse and fall back in. I was out first time but spent. It was over.

The camera rolled for another 30 seconds before the crew came forward and offered their heartfelt congratulations. I felt a great burden instantly lift. There was no more to do. Amazing, then, that in a moment of madness I heard myself agreeing to the director's suggestion that I try to repeat the exercise to see how I fared, because Mawson had taken two attempts to get out of the crevasse into which he fell.

I lowered myself gingerly back into the abyss, still somewhat surprised that I had agreed to be back here again so soon after having climbed out. Mawson had uttered the words of the poet Robert Service 'Just have one more try—it's dead easy to die, it's the keeping-on-living that's hard' like a mantra as he made his final bid for freedom. For me, as clichéd as it sounds, I felt I owed it to Mawson to attempt the crevasse a second time. I looked up. Again, the light at the crevasse mouth seemed distant and unreachable. I sucked in deep lungfuls of air and headed up. This time, I was instantly aware I had little to give. I tired rapidly—and passively accepted the fall, half the rope's length, back down into the bowels of the crevasse, jerking

violently a split second later as I reached the end. I was too tired to care. As I swung in space at the end of the rope I realised what Mawson had achieved in getting out at the second attempt, having narrowly failed at the first.

When I was eventually out, sitting on the snow, exhausted from the experience, John came over to offer congratulations of his own, being able to do so for the first time since his 'death' eighteen days before. Slapping me on the back, he laughed: 'Tonight, we toast the success of your terrible deal'—that now familiar Russian expression, this time mockingly celebrating bad luck that brings good fortune. 'It was a great joint effort', I managed in response.

I removed the Burberry and donned my modern down jacket for the first time in a month and a half, suddenly aware of how little the former had provided in warmth and yet how accustomed to it I had become. It was as if, in wearing the old clothes and assuming the countenance of those explorers of old, there was a certain pride, something to live up to, that helped to steel resolve when things were bleak. They may have travelled in wooden boats, those men of old, but they were iron men—of that there could be no doubt.

Above: *The smiles say it all. A few days after I finished, when food and rest have made my smile broader.*

What followed was a series of shocks to the system: pleasant experiences but shocks nonetheless, with all of the practices I had become accustomed to during the past month and a half completely discarded. The vehicles that effortlessly moved humans around after my prolonged experience of human-powered locomotion; conversations with people congratulating John and me on the toil that was now behind us; phone calls to Elizabeth and my parents; plentiful, nutritious food; the glorious sensation of a hot shower washing away 45 days' worth of accumulated grime from an emaciated body—the rapid procession of change was almost too much after the isolation of the plateau.

Previous page: *The freedom of a chopper ride after the shackles of the sled is almost too much to take in as we fly back to Davis.*

The chopper took off and within minutes the snow and ice of the plateau had given way to the patchwork of mountains, lakes and inlets of the Vestfold Hills. Twenty minutes later we were back at Davis Base, being welcomed by 'Cookie', who—in addition to being the base leader—enjoyed the further distinction of having one of the only cars for thousands of kilometres around. His was a warm welcome and he offered the full services of the base to us for the duration of our stay until the ship arrived in just over a month.

. . .

Epilogue: So This is the End

Shown to my single billet, I closed the door behind me and sat on the bed. The wave of warmth was instantaneous, the incessant wind finally silent, the incredible stillness deafening, as I sat motionless, no longer reliant on movement to generate warmth. I undressed, climbed into crisp, fresh bedding too comfortable to sleep in despite all efforts. My mind raced. Mawson, on finishing, had wanted to spend as much time as possible with people after having lived with the likelihood of a solitary death up on the plateau. However, I relished this quiet time to myself to digest things without the distraction of the toil and constant vigilance that had previously occupied all of my being. Ironically, although I had craved the prospect of peaceful sleep for the past six weeks, now there was no time for it, not yet. There was too much in my head that needed sorting through to sleep.

During the steadily decreasing daylight hours, to clear my head and to stop my stiffening joints and sore muscles from seizing up altogether, I took breaks, walking along the shoreline near the base. The ocean was only 50 metres from my cabin, complete with a colony of noisy elephant seals and spectacular bergs sitting grounded on the ocean bed just offshore.

Previous page: *Looking north towards the mountains of the Vestfolds, which hold back the ice of the plateau. Davis is at the seaward end of this mountain range;*
above left: *A month after finishing and full sensation has returned to my extremities, aided by the spa in the generator room at Davis;*
above centre: *Meeting the Russians at Progress Base and getting a lift in Igor's tank;*
above right: *Winter slowly takes hold at Davis.*

Wonderful crimson and russet-orange sunsets punctuated the end of each day and the occasional green and red swirls of spectacular aurora overhead in the dead of night seemed both magical and designed to inspire. Even the cold katabatic wind obligingly blew to remind me of where I had so recently been and how lucky I was to now be here.

Much of what occupied me was trying to order the multitude of experiences John and I had had, juxtaposing them with those of Mawson and Mertz and trying to make sense of everything.

One of the most obvious and striking differences was Mertz's illness and death. By Day 16 Mawson recorded that Mertz was 'off-colour' and by Day 25 he was dead. In the ten days following Mertz's first symptoms, he experienced rapidly decreasing health, physical strength, enthusiasm for their task and optimism about their chances of success. Mawson felt at the time that Mertz had died of fever but it is curious that his decline came so soon after the loss of the last dog. Much of their slow progress was due to Mertz's physical state and not the weather.

One thing I knew was that Mertz and John toiled in similar conditions to achieve their respective distances, but their experiences were drastically different. Despite the similar conditions, clothing and problems with both wetness and cold, John did not develop Mertz's terrible symptoms. Although John's moods, cold tolerance and judgement were affected or impaired by the conditions, he did not end up dramatically weakened, hallucinating or in

need of medical attention to fend off an even worse fate. The difference leads almost without doubt to the fact that the dog livers and the vitamin A within them must have been a major factor in Mertz's death, but perhaps not the only one.

I tend to feel that Mertz's death was the combined result of several factors that began with the loss of his overtrousers on Ninnis' sled, which meant that, in the heavy snowfall they experienced, he was constantly wet. The seesawing temperatures that subsequently turned this moisture into ice when temperatures dropped made him extremely debilitated, a condition not helped by the wet, cold sleeping conditions (something John and I knew all about too, with sopping-wet sleeping bags of our own). When Mertz finally switched to a diet of more

Above: *The awe-inspiring green swirls of the aurora australis above Davis Base in early March.*

milk and cocoa and less dog meat, it was obviously too late. His level of debilitation in turn led to a greatly reduced resistance to illness, exacerbated by the extra workload of eventually pulling without any dogs, plus the psychological impact of the loss of the final dog, Ginger. All these things contributed to making him a desperately weak, broken man, vulnerable to the ill effects of vitamin A poisoning.

What then allowed Mawson to survive—when Mertz had not—to complete this most incredible of journeys alone? In the first instance, Mawson probably consumed less of the dog livers than Mertz. This is a well-known hypothesis but, although it apparently helps to explain why Mawson was afforded life while Mertz was not, it sheds little light on how Mawson managed to complete his journey. For this, you need to look at their journey more closely.

First, Mawson and Mertz travelled well up until the loss of the last dog—that was definite. Our experience of trying to keep up with Mawson and Mertz's daily averages showed how impossible this was, despite our considerable track record in undertaking expeditions in cold climes. Regardless of our fitness, experience and constant application to the task, John and I were unable to come close to the distances they managed. (This 'headstart' of theirs was almost wiped out by the periods they spent tent-bound with Mertz's ill health and bad weather; we had to rely on Mawson experiencing the bulk of his non-travel days at this mid-point of his journey to claw back the distance such that I ended up on equal terms when John departed.)

Mawson's good initial progress is also supported by another important fact—how little serious consideration he gave to descending to the coast where supplementary food in the form of seals and penguins might have been found. Certainly a fear of what he might find there both in terms of the crevassing and the massive ice cliffs was such that the plateau route, as bad as it was, still represented a shorter and possibly safer route on balance. The two men initially seem to have consumed their rations at a faster rate than we did, indicating that they were anticipating a quicker return journey, a point confirmed by a number of Mawson's diary entries.

They were actually on course to keep to their schedule until Mertz's illness and death. Despite the setbacks, they covered the ground well enough on the plateau for Mawson to have felt

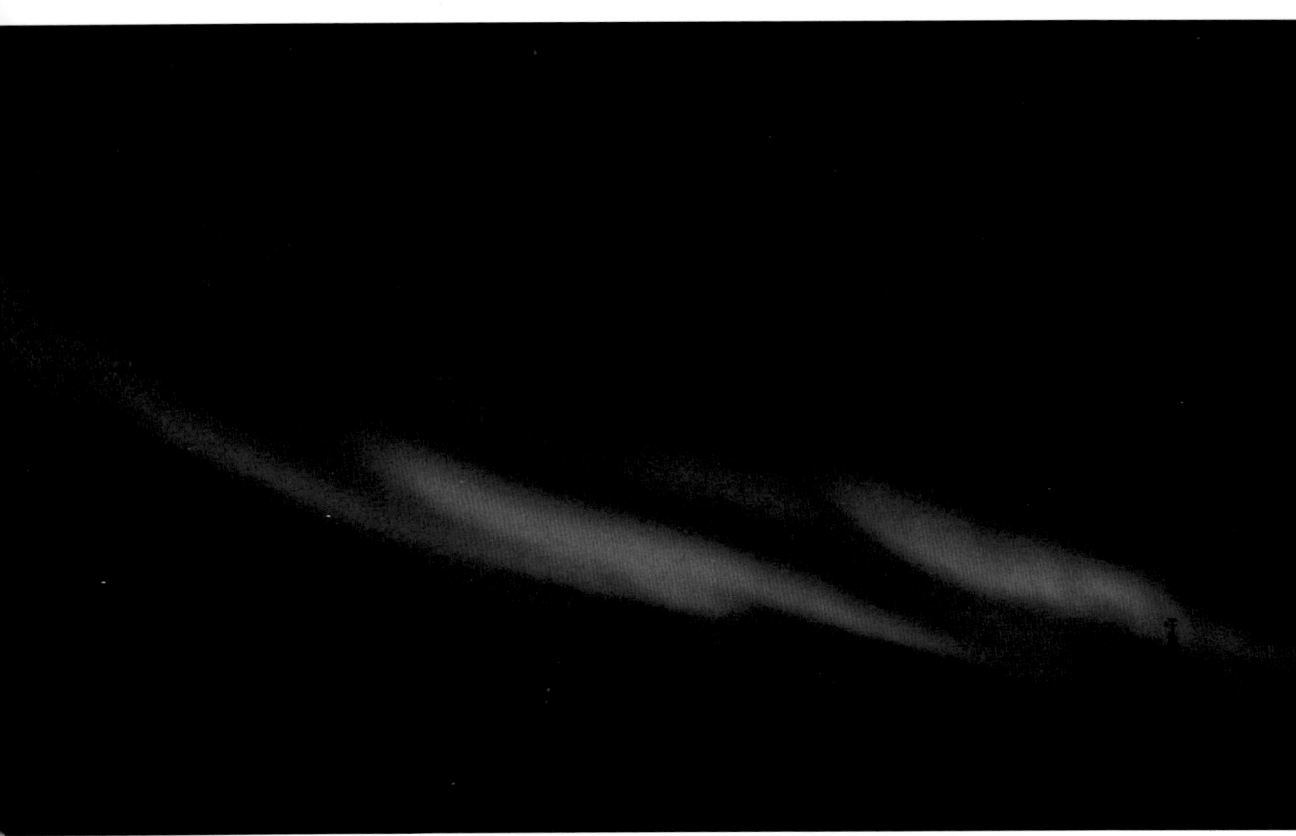

that they need not risk the coastal journey. By the time Mawson realised the impact of Mertz's debilitation, when the coastal route and its possible animal life might have tempted Mawson, Mertz's health was simply too bad to consider attempting it.

Dramatic differences in our experiences certainly began to manifest themselves once Mawson and I were alone on our respective journeys. We both cut our sleds in half without incident, but thereafter our two journeys diverged. Mawson's health declined, with clumps of his hair falling out, painful digestive complaints, weeping sores and whole rafts of skin coming off his feet, whereas I weakened though to nowhere near the same extent. I experienced foot problems, including the onset of frostbite to the toes on my right foot, severe joint

Above: *The green swirls of the aurora ebb and flow like liquid in the night sky.*

pain and some skin loss, plus rawness around the groin from chafing (which lanolin just managed to keep in check), but I did not suffer as much Mawson's diary entries indicate he did. Significantly, my weight did not drop as much as his. Even taking into account the fact that he may have spent longer out in the conditions than I did as he tentatively picked his way through more crevassed terrain—although I added distance to balance this out—other forces were evidently at work. The slow pace of the second half of Mawson's journey was attributable to his inability to use the wind to its full advantage, his understandable concern about crevasses, the heavy, wet snow he encountered on a number of days and his ill health.

And so I gained on Mawson's distances when on my own, continuing the trend that John and I had established during our last week together, enabling me to finish my journey inside Mawson's time with a small amount of food left over. My remaining rations would have allowed me to continue for a further two days or so, knowing that safety awaited me. Had I been tent-bound and forced to make the rations last to match Mawson's forty-seven days, I could have done so. It would have been unpleasant but certainly possible.

When all is said and done, we both covered our respective distances at almost identical average speeds, although I did not suffer physically to the same extent as Mawson. Undoubtedly, he suffered from the effects of vitaminosis just as Mertz had: the symptoms of hair and skin loss, bleeding gums and aching joints are all consistent with the condition. For some reason, whether it was his having consumed less dog liver than Mertz or having a constitution more resistant to its effects, he was able to survive. The dosages at which vitamin A exhibits toxic effects on people vary massively and so it comes as no great surprise to me that someone with as strong a constitution as Mawson, who was also simply a bigger man than Mertz, suffered less.

Is there something else then? If Mawson suffered physically far more than me but still made it, what does it say about his physical and mental fortitude? Certainly he never lost his resolve, although it was tested to its limits. But Mawson did undergo a distinct change as the journey progressed. Initially, he applied his scientific mind and the disciplined approach that scientists must have to planning and executing his remarkable survival bid. With Mertz's decline and death, and Mawson's subsequent near misses with crevasses, his belief appeared to subtly change from one of relying solely on himself and his own resourcefulness and ability, to increasing recognition of external assistance. This he refers to as 'Providence'—and

Providence, I believe, is synonymous with God. Although he may have been a churchgoing man before embarking on the expedition, by the end he appeared to be a true believer. He seemed to derive strength from the powerful combination of belief in himself and a belief that he was destined to succeed with the assistance of some higher force. On their own both were powerful; together they were irrepressible.

And what of rumours of cannibalism that have lurked in the wings for the past century? I lay awake in my bed in the darkness of the Antarctic night listening to the wind howling down from the plateau. My head pounded. It was not difficult to imagine Mawson up there on the plateau right now, lying there beside the cadaver of his fallen colleague and considering his options. Had he felt tempted to eat Mertz's flesh because it might have meant the difference between life and death? In the final analysis, I don't think he seriously considered it. I think he would have been torn between an overwhelming sense of loyalty towards Mertz and a clear, objective appreciation of how narrow his chance of survival was without more food, while wanting to survive to tell the tale of what had happened. In the end, I think loyalty to Mertz would have prevailed and that he buried him beneath snow blocks, erected a crude cross and turned to meet his fate—whatever it might be—just as he said. Perhaps fittingly, the most conclusive support for Mawson's actions comes from the science that he loved so dearly. Even taking into account the fact that Mawson was sick with vitaminosis, his terrible level of debilitation and far greater weight loss than me mean that I simply don't think he could have eaten Mertz's flesh.

What I would say is that I think Mertz's death saved Mawson. The positives of travelling with Mertz as an able-bodied companion, affording safer passage through crevassed areas, greater sled-pulling power and a greater chance to travel on bad-weather days were outweighed by the negatives of his terrible decline and the benefits that his rations provided. Although Mawson's distances slowed when on his own, based on my experiences I attribute this to his poor health and bad weather and not the ability of one man to pull a half-sled as well as two men can pull a full sled. Mertz's death may not have provided literally for Mawson, but certainly his death, as devastating as it was for Mawson at the time, allowed him to live to complete what is surely one of the greatest journeys of human endeavour.

Opposite: *The view from my cabin: the islands and bergs off Davis.*

And what of me: how do I feel? What I know for sure is that, despite pride at having completed my journey, I feel more than anything humbled by it. I have an even greater respect for what Mawson and Mertz achieved. Theirs was without doubt a terrible journey, and one that mine in the modern era could not claim to have replicated. I had done so as closely as I could and that was bad enough. By subjecting myself to a journey similar to that of Mawson and telling his story parallel with mine, I hope it will help bring his ordeal to the attention of the larger audience I believe it deserves, shedding light on the events that unfolded down on the lonely Antarctic plateau—the 'home of the blizzard'—almost 100 years ago.

Appendix: Antarctica under Threat

The hunt for whales and seals for oil was the motivation behind the initial exploration of Antarctic waters in the early nineteenth century. As an industry, Antarctic whaling was conducted much like mining, with no thought to sustainability. Once the most profitable species had been hunted to near extinction or commercial scarcity, the next species was hunted until it too reached similarly low numbers. Southern right whales, common in waters off the Australian coast today when they migrate from their Antarctic feeding grounds, are a good example of this practice. Their numbers were massively reduced during the active years of the whaling industry. Even the right whales' name was due to the whaling industry: they were the 'right' ones to hunt, because they often swam close to shore and they floated when harpooned, making it easy for the whalers to 'harvest' them.

Whales were not the only victims of humanity's exploration of Antarctic and subantarctic waters: seals and even penguins were killed and 'processed' for the oil their bodies contained, and for other products. On Macquarie Island, where Mawson established a base hut and wireless station en route to Antarctica, fur seals were killed for their skins, with the population plummeting from between 200 000 and 400 000 animals to virtually nothing in just a decade.

Once fur seals had been hunted to virtual extinction, sealers turned to elephant seals, killing them and refining their blubber to extract oil for products such as soap and lamp oil. By the mid-1840s elephant seal numbers had been similarly devastated. Sealers then turned their attention to the island's three million penguins. At the height of the industry in 1905, 2000 penguins a day were being processed in 'digesters', with each penguin producing about half a litre of oil.

Penguin harvesting did not go on for long and the International Whaling Commission was set up in 1946 to regulate whaling. But the main factor that led to a reduction in whaling was falling profits—due to a lack of whales because they had been so exhaustively hunted. But conservation efforts slowly began to have an impact. In the 1960s blue and humpback whales became protected; fin and sei whales were protected in the 1970s. In 1986 all commercial whaling was stopped although some nations such as Japan continue to hunt whales for 'scientific purposes'. Once the whale's body has served its scientific purpose, it is sold commercially for massive amounts of money.

The fate of seals was tied up with the fate of Antarctica's second most famous introduced species after humans: sled dogs. Commercial sealing was stopped in the 1950s, although seals were still killed (in relatively small numbers) to feed the dog teams operating in Antarctica up until the early 1990s. But the threat to the seals was not from being killed for dog food; the threat was from distemper, a common disease in dogs. Dogs were outlawed in Antarctica in 1993 because of concern that distemper might spread to seals. The removal of the dogs in turn reduced any further need to kill seals, as there were no dogs to feed.

Illegal longline fishing in Antarctic and subantarctic waters for Patagonian toothfish and other fish with longlines that can be tens of kilometres long unfortunately remains an ongoing problem. Not only do the longlines rapidly eat into the fish stocks but birds such as albatrosses, which feed on the bait as the longlines are being set, get caught on hooks and drown. Illegal fishing fleets are also moving ever closer to the Ross Sea, one of the most pristine places on Earth and one that deserves complete protection from fishing.

Two groups of visitors now regularly visit Antarctica: tourists and people employed on the various national Antarctic bases. Tourists outnumber the others (approximately 35 000 to 4000 in 2006), but both the majority of registered tourism operators and the national bases are careful to maintain the environment. They follow strict codes of practice in regard to wildlife, quarantine regulations, waste management, marine regulations and more. Regardless of this, the more activity there is in Antarctica, the more potential there is for damage to the environment, especially with tourist numbers in particular on the increase.

Despite the harm that humans have caused marine animals in the past and, to a far lesser extent, the impacts associated with tourism and scientific activity in Antarctica today, the biggest threats to Antarctica are not caused by human activities on the continent but by our activities elsewhere. The irony is that Antarctica is likely to return the favour with interest: its ice melt, remotely caused by human-induced global warming, is likely to in turn have massive effects on humanity through global sea-level rises.

THE HEAT IS ON

We now accept the global warming phenomenon, with the role of humanity in contributing significantly to it also now beyond doubt. Even a body as conservative as the United Nations Intergovernmental Panel on Climate Change (IPCC), which, for example, requires all of its published findings be approved by a consensus of more than 300 expert scientists, has produced startling figures on the world's changing atmosphere and climates. That the Panel should unambiguously conclude that global warming is 'very likely' the result of human activity is therefore good reason to feel that the debate is over. The IPCC's fourth Assessment Report in 2007 also contained warnings with particular relevance to Antarctica. It warned that warming of the world's climate was 'unequivocal', with the evidence observable now in increases in the average air and ocean temperatures around the globe and widespread melting of snow and ice. The IPCC also reported that while it is not unusual for the Earth's climate to change over time, the warmth of the past fifty years is unusual against the pattern of the past 1300 years. The past time the polar regions were significantly warmer than they are now—about 125 000 years ago—sea levels rose 4 to 6 metres due to reductions in the amount of ice at the poles.

The most significant impact of global warming for Antarctica is ice melt, with its implications for sea levels and world weather patterns. The extent to which the volume of Antarctic ice changes is determined by a number of factors, but the two most significant are the flow rate of glaciers towards the sea and the rate of accumulation of snow over Antarctica through snowfall.

Global warming may, on the one hand, be increasing the moisture content of the atmosphere and in turn increasing snowfall over parts of Antarctica. On the other hand, there is the increased speed at which glaciers around Antarctica are flowing to the sea, due to lubrication of their bases by water from ice melt.

The interplay of these factors affects both 'parts' of Antarctica, and I use this term because Antarctica is divided into two caps or ice sheets: West Antarctic Ice Sheet (WAIS) and East Antarctic Ice Sheet (EAIS). The larger EAIS is approximately 23 million cubic kilometres in size and is entirely above sea level, covering 'Greater Antarctica'; the smaller WAIS is situated on rock at or just below sea level to the west of the Transantarctic Mountains. The two combined account for some 28 million cubic kilometres of ice—90 per cent of the world's ice.

If the EAIS were to melt entirely, it would cause sea levels around the world to rise by some 50–55 metres. This is because virtually all of the ice in this cap is situated on land; when it melts, all of the water it contains will move from being on land to the sea, raising sea levels.

The WAIS, some 5 million cubic kilometres in size, is a marine-based ice sheet, meaning that its bed lies below sea level and its edges flow into floating ice shelves. This includes the Ross and Ronne ice shelves (which form the boundaries of the WAIS) and glaciers that drain into the Amundsen Sea.

Sceptics of climate change commonly downplay the significance of the WAIS melting by arguing that, because this sheet is floating already, it is already displacing its own volume in water and therefore its melting will not directly affect sea levels, in the same way that the level of a drink does not increase when an ice cube melts in it. While there is some truth in this particular point, the melting of the WAIS will have other serious effects. First, melting sea-ice speeds up glacier flow-rates, causing more rapid shedding of land-based ice into the sea; this would cause considerable rises in sea levels. Second, parts of the WAIS are not floating in water; instead, they are part of a massive weight of ice that actually rests on the sea bed, supporting a large amount of ice that is currently above sea level. When this melts, it will cause sea levels to rise. Finally, other ice from the WAIS on land below sea level is melting; it too will contribute to a sea-level rise when the sea ice that currently pens it melts away. And if all of the WAIS melted, it would cause a rise in the world's sea levels of around 5 metres.

THE TIPPING POINT

The Larsen B Ice Shelf (3250 square kilometres in area and 200 metres thick) broke up in less than a month in 2002 and is a good example of the glacier acceleration problem. Ice shelves like the Larsen B form the floating edge of ice sheets that extend out into the sea. When they break apart, they do not directly cause sea levels to rise but they do dramatically increase the speed of ice loss from glaciers behind them.

Larsen B is just one event in a trend of increased ice loss from the WAIS and the Antarctic Peninsula that scientists have observed over the past decade or so. A report by Professor Jonathan Bamber and colleagues from Bristol University, published online recently in *Nature Geoscience*, revealed a best estimate loss of 132 billion tonnes of ice in 2006 from West Antarctica—up from about 83 billion tonnes in 1996—and a loss of about 60 billion tonnes in 2006 from the Antarctic Peninsula, most of which was due to increased speed of glacier flow and calving.

To put things in perspective, the UK's total annual water consumption is just 4 billion tonnes. Some scientists now feel that there is a real chance this ice sheet may reach a tipping point and collapse altogether. If it does, ocean levels would rise massively in a very short period of time, giving us hardly any time to adapt.

The ice mass in the EAIS is reportedly roughly stable, with neither loss nor growth occurring, because increased speed of glacier calving is being offset by increased snow accumulation. But the thinning of potentially vulnerable marine ice around the coast of East Antarctica suggests this may change in the near future, resulting in increased speed of glacier calving as is happening in the WAIS and Antarctic Peninsula and causing far greater sea-level rises than we are currently seeing.

Global sea levels in the meantime are estimated to have risen by 1.8 millimetres a year on average during the twentieth century. Data from the past decade or so suggests that the average rise has increased to about 3.4 millimetres a year. In contrast, from 3000 years ago to the start of the nineteenth century, sea-level rise was almost constant, rising at 0.1 to 0.2 millimetres a year.

With sea-level rises some of the issues we will face increasingly between now and 2100 include the massive loss of agricultural land and contamination of freshwater aquifers due to saltwater inundation; loss of urban space and productive land in cities; inundation of low-lying land, consisting of not only many of the world's major coastal cities, but also, and perhaps more worryingly, large population centres in low-lying developing countries such as China and Bangladesh. The latter potentially will result in hundreds of millions of environmental refugees who need to migrate to new areas to survive.

There will be massive costs associated with construction of coastal defences, a big burden placed upon the insurance industry and increased costs associated with food production, all of which will inevitably be passed on to business and the consumer. And with such vast numbers of the world's population currently situated in low-lying coastal regions, not to mention many of the world's cities such as Jakarta, London, New York, Amsterdam, Mumbai and Shanghai—and all of Australia's state capitals—to name but a few, the social and economic implications for humanity alone will be enormous.

OZONE HOLE

Ozone is a form of oxygen that blocks out hazardous ultraviolet (UV) light rays from the sun but allows visible light and warm infrared rays to pass through. Life on Earth relies on the presence of a thin layer of ozone, from about 15 to 40 kilometres up in the atmosphere, for protection from UV radiation that can damage DNA as well as producing tumours and cancers in humans and causing cataracts.

In the mid-1970s, scientists noticed that chlorine produced in the atmosphere from the human-made chlorofluorocarbons (CFCs) used in refrigerators, fire extinguishers, air conditioners and aerosols was building up in the atmosphere and depleting the ozone layer.

The most dramatic discovery came in the mid-1980s when the British Antarctic Survey discovered an enormous ozone hole. The extremely low temperatures that occurred over Antarctica each winter meant that the CFCs in the atmosphere broke down, forming chlorine, which in turn reacted with and destroyed ozone.

In a bid to combat this phenomenon, a multilateral agreement was signed in 1987 by the United Nations: the Montreal Protocol. It resulted in a staged phase-out and ultimate ban on the use of CFCs and related chemicals. Although that was a great initiative, CFCs will unfortunately remain with us for some time to come. Particularly cold winters, such as that of 2006, still result in large ozone holes in the atmosphere because of the role that extreme cold plays in turning the CFCs left in the atmosphere into ozone-depleting chlorine. As a result of action taken by governments around the world, however, ozone-depleting gases in the atmosphere are now increasing less rapidly and the situation is slowly but surely improving.

The Montreal Protocol is a successful multilateral response to an international problem and a positive example that could be applied usefully to larger issues such as global warming.

MANAGING ANTARCTICA

Since its inception, the Antarctic treaty system has provided an effective means of managing Antarctica. In 1958, eighteen countries, seven of which had a territorial stake in the region—Australia, Argentina, Chile, France, New Zealand, Norway and the UK—signed the original Antarctic Treaty. The original treaty recognised Antarctica as a unique scientific and planetary resource for the whole of humankind and protected it for thirty years. The Protocol on Environmental Protection to the Antarctic Treaty (Environmental Protocol or Madrid Protocol) was agreed in 1991 and came into force in 1998.

Those who signed the Madrid Protocol have committed themselves to the 'comprehensive protection of the Antarctic environment'. The Protocol sets out principles for environmental protection and bans all mining or commercial mineral resource activity. Instead, it sees Antarctica as a 'natural reserve, devoted to peace and science'. Significantly, all activities in Antarctica must have an environmental impact assessment before they are allowed to go ahead.

The Protocol also covers, among other things, conservation measures for Antarctic plants and animals, how to prevent marine pollution and, at a more basic yet practical level, what should be done about waste disposal and management.

Although there are challenges to this legal regime, posed by issues such as climate change, tourism and fishing and whaling in the Southern Ocean, the Antarctic Treaty system is proving a good way to manage Antarctica as a global resource for all of humanity. Things have come a long way in one hundred years and Mawson would surely have approved.

Picture Credits

Unless otherwise indicated, all images are supplied by the author.

p. v Courtesy of John Stoukalo.

Introduction
p. 1 Courtesy of John Stoukalo; p. 2 Frank Hurley, National Library of Australia; p. 5 (left) unknown photographer, National Library of Australia; p. 5 (right) Frank Hurley, Mitchell Library, State Library of New South Wales; p. 7 Map by Martin Von Wyss; pp. 8–9 Courtesy of John Stoukalo; pp. 10–11 Frank Hurley, Mitchell Library, State Library of New South Wales; p. 13 Xavier Mertz, Mitchell Library, State Library of New South Wales; p. 14 Courtesy of John Stoukalo; p. 17 Map by Martin Von Wyss.

1   Arrival
pp. 18–19, 22–3, 27 Courtesy of John Stoukalo; p. 28 *Mawson: Life and Death in Antarctica*. 2007. Stills supplied by Film Australia. Photograph by Malcolm McDonald; pp. 30 (bottom), 31, 32 (top), 36–7 Courtesy of John Stoukalo.

2   The Plateau
p. 43 Courtesy of Malcolm McDonald; p. 46 (left) Courtesy of John Stoukalo; pp. 46 (right), 47, 48–9, 51, 54–5, 57, 61, 63 Courtesy of Malcolm McDonald.

3   Stopka
p. 70 Xavier Mertz, Mitchell Library, State Library of New South Wales; pp. 75, 76–7 Courtesy of Malcolm McDonald; pp. 79 (left), 81 Courtesy of John Stoukalo.

4   Wind Power
pp. 82–3, 85 Courtesy of John Stoukalo; pp. 86–7 Courtesy of Malcolm McDonald; p. 88 *Mawson: Life and Death in Antarctica*. 2007. Stills supplied by Film Australia. Photograph by Frederique Olivier; p. 91 Courtesy of John Stoukalo; p. 92 Xavier Mertz, Mitchell Library, State Library of New South Wales; pp. 93, 96–7, 98 Courtesy of Malcolm McDonald; p. 99 Frank Hurley, Mitchell Library, State Library of New South Wales; p. 101 Courtesy of John Stoukalo.

5 Losing a Friend

p. 105 Courtesy of Malcolm McDonald; pp. 107 (right), 109 Courtesy of John Stoukalo; p. 111 Xavier Mertz, Mitchell Library, State Library New South Wales; pp. 112, 115, 121, 122–3 Courtesy of Malcolm McDonald.

6 Alone on the Shores of the World

pp. 124–5, 127, 128, 130–1 Courtesy of Malcolm McDonald; pp. 134–5 *Mawson: Life and Death in Antarctica*. 2007. Stills supplied by Film Australia. Photograph by Frederique Olivier; p. 137 Frank Hurley, National Library of Australia; pp. 138, 145 Courtesy of Malcolm McDonald.

7 False Start

pp. 148–9, 151, 154–5 Courtesy of Malcolm McDonald; pp. 156, 159 Courtesy of John Stoukalo.

8 Climbing

pp. 160–1 Courtesy of John Stoukalo; pp. 164–5 Courtesy of Malcolm McDonald; pp. 170–1 Courtesy of John Stoukalo; p. 181 Courtesy of Malcolm McDonald; p. 183 (bottom) Courtesy of John Stoukalo.

9 Iceberg Alley

pp. 184–5, 191 Courtesy of Malcolm McDonald; pp. 192–3 *Mawson: Life and Death in Antarctica*. 2007. Stills supplied by Film Australia. Photograph by Malcolm McDonald.

10 'Just Have One more Try—It's Dead Easy to Die'

pp. 198–9, 201, 204–5, 206–7, 209, 210, 211, 213 Courtesy of Malcolm McDonald.

Epilogue: So This is the End

pp. 214–15, 218–19 Courtesy of Malcolm McDonald; pp. 220–1 Courtesy of John Stoukalo; p. 222 *Mawson: Life and Death in Antarctica*. 2007. Stills supplied by Film Australia. Photograph by Malcolm McDonald; pp. 224, 227 Courtesy of John Stoukalo.

Appendix: Antarctica under Threat

pp. 231, 232, 233, 235 Courtesy of John Stoukalo.

Acknowledgements

There are many thanks to give and so little space in which to offer them! In particular I'd like to thank the following:

The Honourable Alexandra Shackleton and the Honourable John Howard, former Prime Minister of Australia, for providing joint patronage of the trip.

My expedition partner, John 'Rusky' Stoukalo. Our journey was truly a joint effort and my success is also his success. 'Dai bog ne poslednyaya.'

All at Film Australia, and in particular Executive Producer Alex West, for having confidence in the program and supporting it wholeheartedly.

Ralph Lee at Channel 4 and Stuart Menzies at the ABC for co-funding the program.

My employers URS Ltd, who continue to support my endeavours, and in particular John Gillett. URS is the world's largest environmental consulting firm and supports my expeditions not only as part of their 'employer of choice' program but also because these expeditions promote an important environmental message.

Richard Dennison, my business partner and the creative force behind helping mould the plan for the trip into a television script proposal that became a reality.

The Australian Antarctic Division (AAD), without whom we would never have made it to Antarctica (or back!), and in particular the Director Dr Tony Press, Deputy Director Virginia Mudie, General Manager Operations Kim Pitt, Station Support Coordinator Michael Carr and of course the tireless Rob Easther.

Mark Pharaoh, who unstintingly provided help and support in researching the details of all aspects of Sir Douglas Mawson's journey as curator of the Mawson Collection at the South Australian Museum and as a good friend.

'The crew': Malcolm McDonald (director), Frederique (sound), Wade (camera) and Dr David Tingay (doctor) for their skill and expertise in filming this epic journey so wonderfully.

Graham Cook, aka 'Cookie', base leader at Davis Base 2006–07, and all of the base staff; Frank, Dave and Ricardo from Helicopter Services, accomplished pilots all.

All those who helped us assemble the gear required to mount the expedition, including Andy Chianchi, Perry Stapleton, Chris Block and Mark Thomson for the replica gear they so faithfully recreated; Elisa Bell for researching and sourcing our food; Jaeger for jumpers, woollen thermals and scarves; and Burberry for the 'heroic era' outer layers.

Friends, supporters and advisers who have shared in the effort of making this project a reality. Particular thanks go to Harry Bardwell, Professor Mark Carroll, Roger Daynes, Anne Hurley, Professor Mike Innes, Evie Ledger, Dave Mannix, Dr Andrew McCainch, Greg Mortimer, Michael Morton, Colin Putt, Dr Don Richards and Alexandra Stoukalo. Special thanks to Hannah Mornement, great-great-niece of Ninnis, and Emma McEwin, great-granddaughter of Sir Douglas Mawson.

All at Melbourne University Publishing, in particular Publisher Elisa Berg and editors Susan Keogh and Eugenie Baulch, for all their help.

Last but not least, I would like to thank Elizabeth, who will be my wife by the time this book goes to press. She has been a great support to me before, during and since the expedition, and I have the trip to thank for helping me make the decision to ask her to marry me on my return.

THE MIEGUNYAH PRESS

This book was designed and typeset by Nada Backovic
The text was set in 11.5 point Granjon with 16 points of leading
The text is printed on 130 gsm satin art paper
This book was edited by Susan Keogh